DR BARBARA' LOST
Diabetic Cookbook

Barbara O'Neil's 28-Day Mean Plan & Natural Recipes Reversing Diabetes

Alina Cobb

Copyright © 2024 by Alina Cobb

All rights reserved. No part of this publication may be reproduced, distributed, or transmitted in any form or by any means, including photocopying, recording, or other electronic or mechanical methods, without the prior written permission of the publisher, except in the case of brief quotations embodied in critical reviews and certain other noncommercial uses permitted by copyright law.

This book is intended for personal use and educational purposes only. It is not permitted for resale or commercial distribution without the express permission of the copyright holder.

For permissions requests, inquiries, or other questions regarding this book, please contact:

For permission requests or inquiries, please contact the author at info@farmwella.com

Cover design by Audrey Fox
Printed in the United States

Disclaimer

The information provided in this book, "Dr Barbara Lost Diabetic Cookbook - Barbara O'Neil's 28-Day Mean Plan & Natural Recipes Reversing Diabetes" is for educational and informational purposes only. It is not intended as a substitute for professional medical advice or treatment. Always seek the advice of your physician or other qualified healthcare provider with any questions regarding a medical condition.

While we have made every effort to ensure the accuracy and completeness of the content, we do not guarantee the reliability, suitability, or effectiveness of the recipes, suggestions, or dietary guidelines presented herein. The author, publisher, and contributors are not liable for any personal injury, damage, or loss arising from the use of the information presented in this book. Readers are responsible for their own health and should consult with a healthcare professional before making any dietary or lifestyle changes. The recipes and meal plans in this book are intended to promote healthy aging and well-being, but individual results may vary.

It's important to consult with a qualified healthcare professional or nutritionist before making significant changes to your diet or lifestyle, especially if you have existing health conditions, allergies, or dietary restrictions.

The recipes and dietary recommendations in this book are based on general principles of nutrition and healthy eating. Individual nutritional needs may vary, and what works well for one person may not be suitable for another.

We disclaim any liability for any loss, injury, or damage incurred as a result of the use or misuse of the information provided in this book. Readers are encouraged to use their own judgment and discretion when applying the content to their personal dietary and health practices.

By using this book, you agree that you are responsible for your own health decisions and understand that the information provided is not a substitute for professional medical advice or treatment. Always seek the advice of a qualified healthcare provider with any questions or concerns you may have regarding your health or dietary needs.

Table of CONTENTS

Chapter One - Introduction... 06

Chapter Two - Barbara O'Neil Principles for Managing Diabetes............. 08

Chapter Three - Diabetic Friendly Breakfast Recipes............................. 12
- Spinach and Feta Omelette
- Avocado and Egg Breakfast Bowl
- Quinoa Breakfast Skillet
- Greek Yogurt with Nuts and Seeds
- Mushroom and Spinach Breakfast Burrito
- Spinach and Mushroom Egg Scramble
- Quinoa Breakfast Bowl
- Greek Yogurt with Nuts and Seeds
- Avocado and Egg Rye Toast
- Chickpea and Veggie Breakfast Hash
- Smoked Salmon and Avocado Bowl
- Spicy Black Bean and Egg Breakfast Wrap
- Lentil and Spinach Breakfast Stew
- Tofu Scramble with Vegetables
- Spelt Flour Savory Pancakes
- Kamut and Vegetable Stir-Fry
- Egg and Vegetable Muffins
- Oatmeal with Savory Toppings
- Breakfast Stuffed Bell Peppers
- Baked Avocado with Egg
- Broccoli and Cheese Breakfast Casserole
- Cauliflower Breakfast Rice
- Quinoa Breakfast Bowl
- Millet Porridge with Spinach and Mushrooms
- Buckwheat Breakfast Bowl
- Chia Seed Pudding with Almonds and Berries
- Savory Amaranth Breakfast Porridge
- Sweet Potato and Black Bean Breakfast Hash
- Spinach and Tofu Scramble
- Farro and Vegetable Breakfast Bowl

Chapter Four - Diabetic Friendly Lunch Recipes..................................... 28
- Quinoa and Black Bean Salad
- Lentil and Vegetable Soup
- Spelt Berry and Veggie Bowl
- Chickpea and Spinach Stew
- Brown Rice and Veggie Stir-Fry
- Quinoa Stuffed Bell Peppers
- Spinach and Feta Stuffed Mushrooms
- Mediterranean Chickpea Salad
- Baked Salmon with Quinoa and Asparagus
- Black Bean and Avocado Wrap
- Kale & Quinoa Salad with Lemon-Tahini Dressing
- Spelt and Lentil Pilaf
- Avocado and Chickpea Stuffed Sweet Potatoes
- Brown Rice and Veggie Sushi Rolls
- Greek Yogurt Parfait with Berries and Nuts
- Roasted Veggie and Hummus Bowl
- Greek Yogurt Parfait with Berries and Nuts
- Roasted Veggie and Hummus Bowl
- Curried Chickpea and Spinach Stew
- Quinoa and Black Bean Stuffed Tomatoes

Chapter Five - Diabetic Friendly Salad Recipes....................................... 39
- Quinoa and Black Bean Salad
- Spinach and Chickpea Salad
- Lentil and Vegetable Salad
- Avocado and Kale Salad
- Greek Yogurt and Cucumber Salad
- Brown Rice and Edamame Salad
- Spelt and Avocado Salad
- Roasted Beet and Lentil Salad
- Mediterranean Chickpea Salad
- Farro and Arugula Salad

Chapter Six - Diabetic Friendly Soup Recipes.. 45
- Lentil and Spinach Soup
- Quinoa and Vegetable Soup
- Chicken and Vegetable Soup
- Butternut Squash and Red Lentil Soup
- Black Bean and Quinoa Soup
- Tomato and White Bean Soup
- Chickpea and Spinach Soup
- Kale and Cannellini Bean Soup
- Broccoli and Almond Soup
- Carrot and Ginger Soup
- Mushroom and Barley Soup
- Kale and White Bean Soup
- Sweet Potato and Black Bean Soup
- Zucchini and Chickpea Soup

Chapter Seven – Diabetic Friendly Snacks Recipes 53
- Almond Butter and Celery Sticks
- Greek Yogurt with Chia Seeds and Berries
- Avocado and Black Bean Salsa
- Spiced Roasted Chickpeas
- Spiced Chickpea and Avocado Toast
- Greek Yogurt with Nuts and Seeds
- Spiced Roasted Nuts
- Edamame Hummus with Veggie Sticks

Chapter Eight – Diabetic Friendly Desserts Recipes 58
- Chia Seed Pudding with Berries
- Avocado Chocolate Mousse
- Coconut Yogurt Parfait
- Baked Apple with Cinnamon and Almonds
- Lemon Blueberry Yogurt Bark
- Almond Flour Chocolate Chip Cookies
- Chia Seed Pudding with Berries
- Avocado Chocolate Mousse
- Coconut Flour Lemon Bars
- Cinnamon Walnut Baked Apples
- Berry Yogurt Parfait
- Almond Flour Pumpkin Muffins

Chapter Nine – Diabetic Friendly Dinner Recipes 65
- Grilled Lemon Herb Chicken with Quinoa
- Spaghetti Squash with Turkey Bolognese
- Lentil and Vegetable Stew
- Baked Salmon with Asparagus and Quinoa
- Stuffed Bell Peppers with Ground Beef
- Chickpea and Spinach Curry
- Baked Cod with Tomato and Olive Relish
- Quinoa-Stuffed Portobello Mushrooms
- Turkey and Spinach Stuffed Bell Peppers
- Lemon Herb Grilled Chicken with Brown Rice
- Quinoa & Black Bean Stuffed Sweet Potatoes
- Garlic Shrimp and Zucchini Noodles
- Moroccan-Spiced Chickpea and Spinach Stew
- Baked Tilapia with Tomato Basil Sauce
- Chicken and Vegetable Stir-Fry
- Spiced Lentil and Sweet Potato Stew

Chapter Ten – Diabetic Friendly Fish and Seafood Recipes 74
- Grilled Salmon with Avocado Salsa
- Lemon Garlic Shrimp Stir-Fry
- Baked Cod with Quinoa and Kale
- Tuna and Chickpea Salad
- Mediterranean Baked Halibut
- Shrimp and Vegetable Skewers
- Seared Scallops with Quinoa Pilaf
- Herb-Crusted Baked Tilapia
- Spicy Grilled Mackerel with Brown Rice
- Coconut Curry Shrimp with Cauliflower Rice

Chapter Eleven – Diabetic Friendly Poultry Recipes 80
- Lemon Herb Grilled Chicken
- Baked Chicken and Quinoa Stuffed Peppers
- Chicken Avocado Salad
- Spicy Chicken Lettuce Wraps
- Coconut Curry Chicken
- Balsamic Glazed Chicken with Roasted Vegetables
- Chicken and Vegetable Stir-Fry
- Herb-Roasted Chicken Thighs
- Chicken and Lentil Soup
- Mediterranean Chicken Bake

Chapter Twelve – Barbara Lost Diabetic 30-Day Meal Plan, ... 86
Grocery List and Shopping Guide

Chapter Thirteen – Conclusion 93

Index 94

Index 1: The 2024 Dirty Dozen™ and Clean Fifteen™
Index 2: Measurement Conversions
Index 3: Recipe Index

Chapter One

Introduction

Imagine waking up each morning with a sense of dread about what the day holds for your health—the constant battle to manage your blood sugar levels, the fear of sudden spikes, and the relentless cravings that seem impossible to resist. For many Americans living with diabetes, this is a daily reality.

But what if there were a way to turn this around? What if you could start each day with confidence, knowing that your meals are not just delicious but also designed to help you manage your diabetes effectively? This is the inspiration behind "Dr. Barbara Lost Diabetic Cookbook - Barbara O'Neil's 28-Day Meal Plan & Natural Recipes Reversing Diabetes." This book is not just a collection of recipes; it's a lifeline for those looking to manage diabetes through natural, practical, and incredibly tasty food choices.

Barbara O'Neil, a renowned health educator, has spent years helping people unlock the body's natural ability to heal itself through diet and lifestyle changes. Her philosophy is simple yet profound: with the right foods, our bodies can maintain balance and health without relying on medications alone. This cookbook distills her wisdom into a 28-Day meal plan designed to keep your glucose levels steady, curb cravings, and ensure you have consistent energy throughout the day.

In today's fast-paced world, finding time to cook healthy meals can be a challenge. But Barbara's recipes are easy to follow and use ingredients that are readily available. Whether you're a busy professional, a parent juggling multiple responsibilities, or simply someone looking to improve your health, these recipes are designed with you in mind.

What makes this cookbook truly special is its inclusion of some of Barbara O'Neil's most treasured recipes—ones that can no longer be found online. These recipes have been meticulously curated to ensure that her invaluable insights remain accessible to everyone. Whether you're new to her teachings or have been a follower for years, this book offers a fresh perspective and a practical approach to managing diabetes.

"Dr. Barbara Lost Diabetic Cookbook - Barbara O'Neil's 28-Day Meal Plan & Natural Recipes Reversing Diabetes" isn't just for those with diabetes. It's for anyone seeking a healthier, more balanced lifestyle. In today's fast-paced world, where convenience often trumps nutrition, this cookbook offers a refreshing approach. It's about making mindful choices that support your body's natural ability to thrive.

So, whether you're managing diabetes, or simply looking to improve your overall health, this cookbook is your guide. With chapters dedicated to diabetic-friendly breakfast recipes, lunch recipes, salad recipes, soup recipes, snack recipes, dessert recipes, dinner recipes, fish and seafood recipes, and poultry based recipes.

Who is Barbara O'Neil?

Barbara O'Neil is a name that resonates with millions of health enthusiasts and individuals seeking natural wellness solutions around the globe. Known for her authentic and straightforward approach, Barbara has garnered a dedicated following through her educational videos and lectures. Her work spans various health topics, but she is particularly renowned for her insights into natural remedies and holistic health practices.

Born in the 1960s, Barbara O'Neil's journey to becoming a health educator and naturopath is both diverse and inspiring. She began her professional life as a hairdresser and later transitioned into psychiatric nursing. The 1970s saw her embracing the counterculture movement, living as a hippie, and eventually birthing six children. Her personal experiences, combined with a deep-seated passion for natural health, led her to study naturopathy and nutrition. She also became a stepmother to two more children and served as a health director at two prominent health and wellness retreats in Australia. Barbara's vast life experiences and hands-on approach to health and wellness have made her a beloved figure and a sought-after speaker both in Australia and internationally.

Barbara O'Neil's philosophy centers on the body's innate ability to heal itself when provided with the right conditions. She believes in empowering individuals with knowledge so they can make informed decisions about their health. According to Barbara, the natural world offers a plethora of remedies that, when used correctly, can promote healing without the harmful side effects often associated with mainstream treatments. Her teachings emphasize the importance of a balanced diet, the avoidance of processed foods, and the inclusion of natural, nutrient-rich ingredients. Barbara's approach is holistic, considering the physical, mental, and spiritual aspects of health.

In 2019, Barbara O'Neil faced significant controversy when the New South Wales Health Care Complaints Commission (HCCC) banned her for life from providing free or paid health services. The HCCC investigation concluded that Barbara lacked formal health-related qualifications, including degrees, diplomas, or memberships in accredited health organizations. This decision sparked a debate about the validity and safety of alternative health practices. Critics argue that her methods lack scientific backing and could potentially harm individuals who forgo conventional medical treatments. However, her supporters claim that Barbara's practical advice and natural remedies have positively impacted their lives, emphasizing her authenticity and genuine care for people's well-being.

Barbara O'Neil's journey from a hairdresser to a globally recognized health educator is a testament to her dedication and passion for natural health. Despite the controversies and challenges she has faced, Barbara continues to inspire and educate individuals on the importance of holistic wellness and the body's remarkable ability to heal itself.

"Dr. Barbara's Lost Diabetic Cookbook" encapsulates her philosophy and offers practical, easy-to-follow recipes designed to help manage diabetes and promote overall health. Inside are some recipes from the teaching of Barbara O'Neil for diabetes management that can no longer be found online. Whether you are new to her teachings or a longtime follower, this cookbook is a valuable resource for anyone looking to embrace a healthier, more balanced lifestyle. Join us on this journey towards better health and wellness with the wisdom and guidance of Barbara O'Neil.

Chapter Two

Barbara O'Neil Principles for Managing Diabetes

One of the most compelling aspects of Barbara O'Neil's work is her approach to managing diabetes. She advocates for dietary and lifestyle changes that can help stabilize blood sugar levels and reduce the risk of complications associated with diabetes. Barbara emphasizes the importance of low-glycemic foods, high fiber intake, and the avoidance of refined sugars and genetically modified ingredients. Her diabetes management strategy includes incorporating alternative grains, legumes, and healthy fats into the diet, which aligns with her overarching philosophy of natural and holistic health. Through her teachings, Barbara aims to help individuals achieve steady energy levels and reduce cravings, ultimately supporting better blood sugar management and overall health.

Barbara O'Neil's principles emphasize the importance of diet and lifestyle in managing chronic conditions such as diabetes. In this chapter, we delve into Barbara O'Neil's key principles for maintaining a healthy life, particularly focusing on dietary choices that can help manage blood sugar levels and promote overall well-being.

No Wheat-Based Foods

One of Barbara O'Neil's fundamental principles is to eliminate all forms of wheat-based foods from your diet. This includes common staples such as bread, cereal, pasta, cakes, and pizza. Wheat contains gluten, which can cause inflammation and digestive issues in many individuals. Moreover, wheat-based products often have a high glycemic index, leading to rapid spikes in blood sugar levels, which is detrimental for individuals managing diabetes.
Instead of wheat, O'Neil encourages the use of alternative grains that are not only gluten-free but also have a lower glycemic index. This shift helps stabilize blood sugar levels, reduce inflammation, and improve digestive health. By removing wheat-based foods from your diet, you can avoid sudden glucose spikes and maintain more consistent energy levels throughout the day.

Alternative Grains to Wheat

Barbara O'Neil advocates for the inclusion of alternative grains such as rye, oats, spelt, einkorn, brown rice (cooked fresh every day), quinoa, and kamut. These grains offer a wealth of nutritional benefits and are less likely to cause the blood sugar spikes associated with wheat.

- Rye: Rich in fiber and nutrients, rye helps regulate blood sugar levels and supports digestive health.
- Oats: A great source of soluble fiber, oats can help reduce cholesterol levels and improve heart health.
- Spelt and Einkorn: Ancient grains that are more nutrient-dense and easier to digest than modern wheat.
- Brown Rice: A whole grain that provides essential vitamins and minerals, and has a lower glycemic index compared to white rice.
- Quinoa: A complete protein containing all nine essential amino acids, quinoa is also high in fiber and minerals.
- Kamut: Known for its high protein and fiber content, kamut also provides a range of essential nutrients.

Incorporating these grains into your diet can enhance nutritional intake, support steady blood sugar levels, and improve overall health.

Emphasize Low Glycemic Foods

Low glycemic foods, such as berries, grapefruit, and legumes, are central to Barbara O'Neil's dietary recommendations. These foods are digested and absorbed more slowly, resulting in a gradual rise in blood sugar and insulin levels. This is particularly important for managing diabetes and preventing glucose spikes.

- **Berries:** Rich in antioxidants, vitamins, and fiber, berries such as blueberries, strawberries, and raspberries help reduce inflammation and support immune function.
- **Grapefruit:** This citrus fruit is low in calories and high in vitamins A and C, and its low glycemic index helps manage blood sugar levels.
- **Legumes:** Beans, lentils, and chickpeas are excellent sources of protein and fiber, promoting satiety and steady glucose levels.

By focusing on low glycemic foods, you can maintain better control over your blood sugar levels, reduce the risk of diabetes-related complications, and enjoy sustained energy throughout the day.

Avoid Refined Sugars and High Glycemic Foods

Refined sugars and high glycemic index foods are to be avoided according to Barbara O'Neil's principles. These foods cause rapid spikes in blood sugar levels, leading to energy crashes and increased insulin resistance. Common sources of refined sugars include sugary snacks, desserts, and sweetened beverages.

High glycemic foods, such as white bread, white rice, and sugary cereals, should also be limited. These foods are quickly converted into glucose, causing rapid increases in blood sugar levels.

Instead, choose natural sweeteners in moderation, such as stevia or monk fruit, and focus on whole foods that provide natural sweetness, like fruits. Avoiding refined sugars and high glycemic foods helps maintain stable blood sugar levels and reduces the risk of developing insulin resistance.

Avoid Genetically Modified Ingredients

Barbara O'Neil emphasizes the importance of avoiding genetically modified (GM) ingredients. GM foods have been altered at the genetic level to enhance certain traits, such as pest resistance or increased yield. However, the long-term health effects of consuming GM foods are not well understood, and some studies suggest they may contribute to health issues.

Choosing organic and non-GMO products ensures that your food is free from potentially harmful modifications and chemicals. This principle supports not only your health but also environmental sustainability and biodiversity.

Include High Fiber Foods

Legumes are a cornerstone of Barbara O'Neil's dietary principles. Foods like beans, lentils, and chickpeas are rich in protein, fiber, vitamins, and minerals. They provide a steady release of glucose into the bloodstream, helping to manage blood sugar levels effectively.
Legumes are versatile and can be used in a variety of dishes, from soups and stews to salads and side dishes. Including legumes in your diet enhances satiety, supports digestive health, and provides a valuable source of plant-based protein.

Include Healthy Fat

Healthy fats are essential for maintaining satiety and supporting overall health. Barbara O'Neil encourages the consumption of sources of healthy fats, such as avocado, nuts, olive oil, and seeds. These fats help stabilize blood sugar levels, reduce inflammation, and support heart health.

- Avocado: High in monounsaturated fats, avocado is also rich in fiber and essential nutrients.
- Nuts and Seeds: Almonds, chia seeds, and flaxseeds provide healthy fats, protein, and fiber, making them excellent additions to any meal.
- Olive Oil: A staple of the Mediterranean diet, olive oil is known for its anti-inflammatory properties and cardiovascular benefits.

Including healthy fats in your diet helps enhance satiety, supports brain function, and contributes to a balanced and nutritious eating plan.

Barbara O'Neil's principles for a healthy life are grounded in natural, whole foods that promote steady blood sugar levels, reduce inflammation, and support overall well-being. By following these guidelines, you can enjoy delicious, satisfying meals while effectively managing your blood sugar and maintaining optimal health.

Chapter Three

Diabetic Friendly Breakfast Recipes

SPINACH AND FETA OMELETTE

Servings: 2 | Prep Time: 10 mins | Cook Time: 10 mins | Carbs per Serving: 5g

INGREDIENTS

- 4 large eggs
- 1 cup fresh spinach, chopped
- 1/4 cup feta cheese, crumbled
- 1 tbsp olive oil
- Salt and pepper to taste

DIRECTIONS

1. In a bowl, beat the eggs and season with salt and pepper.
2. Heat the olive oil in a non-stick skillet over medium heat.
3. Add the spinach and sauté until wilted.
4. Pour the eggs into the skillet and cook until they start to set.
5. Sprinkle the feta cheese over the eggs and fold the omelette in half.
6. Cook for another 2-3 minutes until the cheese is melted and the omelette is cooked through.
7. Serve hot.

Ingredient Tips:

- Spinach is low in carbohydrates and high in fiber, making it excellent for blood sugar management.
- Feta cheese adds protein and healthy fats to keep you full.

Nutrient Content (per serving):

- Calories: 220
- Total Fat: 17g
- Protein: 14g
- Carbohydrates: 5g
- Sugars: 1g
- Fiber: 1g
- Sodium: 450mg

AVOCADO AND EGG BREAKFAST BOWL

Servings: 2 | Prep Time: 10 mins | Cook Time: 10 mins | Carbs per Serving: 12g

INGREDIENTS

- 1 ripe avocado, diced
- 4 large eggs
- 1/2 cup cherry tomatoes, halved
- 1/4 cup red onion, finely chopped
- 1 tbsp olive oil
- 1 tbsp fresh lemon juice
- Salt and pepper to taste

DIRECTIONS

1. In a skillet, heat the olive oil over medium heat.
2. Crack the eggs into the skillet and cook until desired doneness.
3. In a bowl, combine the avocado, cherry tomatoes, red onion, and lemon juice.
4. Season with salt and pepper.
5. Divide the avocado mixture into two bowls and top each with two eggs.
6. Serve immediately.

Ingredient Tips:

- Avocados are a great source of healthy fats and fiber, which help maintain steady blood sugar levels.
- Eggs provide high-quality protein.

Nutrient Content (per serving):

- Calories: 300
- Total Fat: 24g
- Protein: 13g
- Carbohydrates: 12g
- Sugars: 2g
- Fiber: 7g
- Sodium: 220mg

QUINOA BREAKFAST SKILLET

Servings: 3 | Prep Time: 15 mins | Cook Time: 20 mins | Carbs per Serving: 28g

INGREDIENTS

- 1 cup cooked quinoa
- 1/2 cup black beans, drained and rinsed
- 1/2 cup corn kernels
- 1/2 cup bell peppers, diced
- 1/4 cup red onion, diced
- 2 cloves garlic, minced
- 2 tbsp olive oil
- 3 large eggs
- 1/4 cup cilantro, chopped
- Salt and pepper to taste

DIRECTIONS

1. In a large skillet, heat the olive oil over medium heat.
2. Add the red onion, bell peppers, and garlic. Sauté until softened.
3. Add the black beans, corn, and quinoa to the skillet. Cook until heated through.
4. Make three wells in the mixture and crack an egg into each well.
5. Cover the skillet and cook until the eggs are set.
6. Sprinkle with cilantro and serve.

Ingredient Tips:

- Quinoa is a high-protein grain with a low glycemic index, making it ideal for blood sugar control.
- Black beans provide fiber and protein, contributing to a steady release of glucose.

Nutrient Content (per serving):

- Calories: 350
- Total Fat: 16g
- Protein: 14g
- Carbohydrates: 28g
- Sugars: 3g
- Fiber: 7g
- Sodium: 300mg

GREEK YOGURT WITH NUTS AND SEEDS

Servings: 2 | Prep Time: 5 mins | Cook Time: 0 mins | Carbs per Serving: 10g

INGREDIENTS

- 1 cup 5% fat Greek yogurt
- 2 tbsp chia seeds
- 2 tbsp flaxseeds
- 2 tbsp almonds, chopped
- 1/2 cup mixed berries

DIRECTIONS

1. In a bowl, combine the Greek yogurt, chia seeds, flaxseeds, and almonds.
2. Top with mixed berries.
3. Serve immediately.

Ingredient Tips:

- Greek yogurt is high in protein and healthy fats, which help stabilize blood sugar.
- Chia and flaxseeds are rich in fiber, promoting steady energy levels.

Nutrient Content (per serving):

- Calories: 250
- Total Fat: 15g
- Protein: 14g
- Carbohydrates: 10g
- Sugars: 5g
- Fiber: 8g
- Sodium: 80mg

MUSHROOM AND SPINACH BREAKFAST BURRITO

Servings: 2 | Prep Time: 10 mins | Cook Time: 10 mins | Carbs per Serving: 25g

INGREDIENTS

- 2 large eggs
- 1 cup mushrooms, sliced
- 1 cup fresh spinach
- 1/4 cup feta cheese, crumbled
- 2 large whole-grain tortillas (rye, spelt, or quinoa)
- 1 tbsp olive oil
- Salt and pepper to taste

DIRECTIONS

1. In a skillet, heat the olive oil over medium heat.
2. Add the mushrooms and cook until browned.
3. Add the spinach and cook until wilted.
4. In a bowl, beat the eggs and season with salt and pepper.
5. Pour the eggs into the skillet and scramble with the vegetables.
6. Divide the mixture between the two tortillas, sprinkle with feta cheese, and wrap them into burritos.
7. Serve hot.

Ingredient Tips:

- Whole-grain tortillas provide complex carbohydrates and fiber, helping to manage blood sugar levels.
- Mushrooms and spinach add vitamins, minerals, and fiber.

Nutrient Content (per serving):

- Calories: 300
- Total Fat: 15g
- Protein: 16g
- Carbohydrates: 25g
- Sugars: 2g
- Fiber: 5g
- Sodium: 450mg

SPINACH AND MUSHROOM EGG SCRAMBLE

Servings: 1 | Prep Time: 5 mins | Cook Time: 10 mins | Carbs per Serving: 6g

INGREDIENTS

- 3 large eggs
- 1 cup fresh spinach, chopped
- 1/2 cup mushrooms, sliced
- 1 tbsp olive oil
- Salt and pepper to taste
- 1/4 avocado, sliced (optional)

DIRECTIONS

1. Heat olive oil in a non-stick skillet over medium heat.
2. Add the mushrooms and cook until they start to soften, about 3 minutes.
3. Add the spinach and cook until wilted, about 2 minutes.
4. In a bowl, whisk the eggs with salt and pepper.
5. Pour the eggs into the skillet and scramble with the spinach and mushrooms until fully cooked, about 3-4 minutes.
6. Serve hot with sliced avocado on the side.

Ingredient Tips:

- Spinach: Low glycemic index, high in fiber, helps in managing blood sugar levels.
- Mushrooms: Low in calories, low glycemic index.
- Avocado: High in healthy fats and fiber, promotes satiety.

Nutrient Content (per serving):

- Calories: 240
- Total Fat: 18g
- Protein: 18g
- Carbohydrates: 6g
- Sugars: 2g
- Fiber: 2g
- Sodium: 300mg

QUINOA BREAKFAST BOWL

Servings: 1 | Prep Time: 10 mins | Cook Time: 15 mins | Carbs per Serving: 35g

INGREDIENTS

- 1/2 cup cooked quinoa
- 1/4 cup black beans, rinsed and drained
- 1/2 avocado, diced
- 1/4 cup cherry tomatoes, halved
- 1/4 cup cucumber, diced
- 1 tbsp olive oil
- 1 tbsp lemon juice
- Salt and pepper to taste

DIRECTIONS

1. In a bowl, combine the cooked quinoa, black beans, avocado, cherry tomatoes, and cucumber.
2. Drizzle with olive oil and lemon juice.
3. Season with salt and pepper.
4. Toss to combine and serve immediately.

Ingredient Tips:

- Quinoa: Low glycemic index, high in protein and fiber, helps in managing blood sugar levels.
- Black Beans: High in fiber and protein, promotes steady glucose release.
- Avocado: High in healthy fats and fiber, enhances satiety.

Nutrient Content (per serving):

- Calories: 350
- Total Fat: 20g
- Protein: 10g
- Carbohydrates: 35g
- Sugars: 3g
- Fiber: 10g
- Sodium: 250mg

GREEK YOGURT WITH NUTS AND SEEDS

Servings: 1 | Prep Time: 5 mins | Cook Time: None | Carbs per Serving: 15g

INGREDIENTS

- 1 cup 5% fat Greek yogurt
- 5 almonds, chopped
- 1 tbsp chia seeds
- 1 tbsp flaxseeds
- 1/4 cup mixed berries (optional)

DIRECTIONS

1. In a bowl, add Greek yogurt.
2. Top with chopped almonds, chia seeds, and flaxseeds.
3. Add mixed berries if desired.
4. Serve immediately.

Ingredient Tips:

- Greek Yogurt: High in protein, moderate glycemic index.
- Almonds, Chia Seeds, Flaxseeds: High in healthy fats and fiber, help manage blood sugar levels.
- Mixed Berries: Low glycemic index, add natural sweetness and fiber.

Nutrient Content (per serving):

- Calories: 300
- Total Fat: 18g
- Protein: 20g
- Carbohydrates: 15g
- Sugars: 8g
- Fiber: 5g
- Sodium: 100mg

AVOCADO AND EGG RYE TOAST

Servings: 1 | Prep Time: 5 mins | Cook Time: 5 mins | Carbs per Serving: 25g

INGREDIENTS

- 1 slice rye bread, toasted
- 1/2 avocado, mashed
- 1 large egg
- 1 tsp olive oil
- Salt and pepper to taste

DIRECTIONS

1. Toast the rye bread slice.
2. In a skillet, heat olive oil over medium heat.
3. Crack the egg into the skillet and cook to your desired doneness.
4. Spread mashed avocado on the toasted rye bread.
5. Top with the cooked egg.
6. Season with salt and pepper.
7. Serve immediately.

Ingredient Tips:

- Rye Bread: Lower glycemic index than wheat bread, high in fiber.
- Avocado: High in healthy fats and fiber, promotes satiety.
- Egg: High in protein, helps stabilize blood sugar levels.

Nutrient Content (per serving):

- Calories: 350
- Total Fat: 24g
- Protein: 12g
- Carbohydrates: 25g
- Sugars: 2g
- Fiber: 8g
- Sodium: 200mg

CHICKPEA AND VEGGIE BREAKFAST HASH

Servings: 2 | Prep Time: 10 mins | Cook Time: 10 mins | Carbs per Serving: 30g

INGREDIENTS

- 1 cup canned chickpeas, rinsed and drained
- 1/2 bell pepper, diced
- 1/2 zucchini, diced
- 1/2 red onion, diced
- 1 tbsp olive oil
- 1/2 tsp paprika
- Salt and pepper to taste

DIRECTIONS

1. Heat olive oil in a large skillet over medium heat.
2. Add the red onion and bell pepper, and sauté for 5 minutes.
3. Add the zucchini and chickpeas, and cook for another 5 minutes.
4. Season with paprika, salt, and pepper.
5. Serve hot.

Ingredient Tips:

- Chickpeas: High in fiber and protein, promotes steady glucose release.
- Vegetables: Low glycemic index, high in fiber and vitamins.

Nutrient Content (per serving):

- Calories: 250
- Total Fat: 12g
- Protein: 8g
- Carbohydrates: 30g
- Sugars: 5g
- Fiber: 10g
- Sodium: 200mg

SMOKED SALMON AND AVOCADO BOWL

Servings: 1 | Prep Time: 10 mins | Cook Time: None | Carbs per Serving: 12g

INGREDIENTS

- 2 oz smoked salmon
- 1/2 avocado, sliced
- 1/2 cup cucumber, sliced
- 1/4 cup cherry tomatoes, halved
- 1 tbsp capers
- 1 tbsp olive oil
- 1 tbsp lemon juice
- Salt and pepper to taste

DIRECTIONS

1. In a bowl, arrange the smoked salmon, avocado, cucumber, cherry tomatoes, and capers.
2. Drizzle with olive oil and lemon juice.
3. Season with salt and pepper.
4. Serve immediately.

Ingredient Tips:

- Smoked Salmon: High in protein and omega-3 fatty acids.
- Avocado: High in healthy fats and fiber, promotes satiety.
- Vegetables: Low glycemic index, high in fiber and vitamins.

Nutrient Content (per serving):

- Calories: 350
- Total Fat: 28g
- Protein: 18g
- Carbohydrates: 12g
- Sugars: 4g
- Fiber: 6g
- Sodium: 600mg

SPICY BLACK BEAN AND EGG BREAKFAST WRAP

Servings: 1 | Prep Time: 5 mins | Cook Time: 10 mins | Carbs per Serving: 20g

INGREDIENTS

- 2 large eggs
- 1/2 cup black beans, rinsed and drained
- 1 small bell pepper, diced
- 1 tbsp olive oil
- 1/2 tsp chili powder
- Salt and pepper to taste
- 1 large lettuce leaf or a whole grain tortilla

DIRECTIONS

1. In a skillet, heat olive oil over medium heat.
2. Add the bell pepper and cook for 5 minutes.
3. Add the black beans and chili powder, and cook for another 3 minutes.
4. In a bowl, whisk the eggs with salt and pepper.
5. Pour the eggs into the skillet and scramble with the black beans and bell pepper until fully cooked.
6. Spoon the mixture onto a large lettuce leaf or whole grain tortilla.
7. Wrap and serve immediately.

Ingredient Tips:

- Black Beans: High in fiber and protein, promotes steady glucose release.
- Eggs: High in protein, helps stabilize blood sugar levels.
- Bell Pepper: Low glycemic index, high in vitamins and antioxidants.

Nutrient Content (per serving):

- Calories: 300
- Total Fat: 18g
- Protein: 18g
- Carbohydrates: 20g
- Sugars: 2g
- Fiber: 8g
- Sodium: 400mg

LENTIL AND SPINACH BREAKFAST STEW

Servings: 2 | Prep Time: 10 mins | Cook Time: 10 mins | Carbs per Serving: 25g

INGREDIENTS

- 1/2 cup cooked lentils
- 1 cup fresh spinach, chopped
- 1/2 cup diced tomatoes
- 1/2 small onion, diced
- 1 clove garlic, minced
- 1 tbsp olive oil
- 1/2 tsp cumin
- Salt and pepper to taste

DIRECTIONS

1. Heat olive oil in a pot over medium heat.
2. Add the onion and garlic, and sauté for 3 minutes.
3. Add the diced tomatoes and cumin, and cook for another 2 minutes.
4. Stir in the cooked lentils and spinach.
5. Cook until the spinach is wilted and the stew is heated through, about 5 minutes.
6. Season with salt and pepper.
7. Serve hot.

Ingredient Tips:

- Lentils: High in fiber and protein, promotes steady glucose release.
- Spinach: Low glycemic index, high in vitamins and fiber.
- Tomatoes: Low glycemic index, high in vitamins and antioxidants.

Nutrient Content (per serving):

- Calories: 250
- Total Fat: 10g
- Protein: 12g
- Carbohydrates: 25g
- Sugars: 6g
- Fiber: 10g
- Sodium: 300mg

TOFU SCRAMBLE WITH VEGETABLES

Servings: 2 | Prep Time: 10 mins | Cook Time: 10 mins | Carbs per Serving: 12g

INGREDIENTS

- 1/2 block firm tofu, crumbled
- 1/2 bell pepper, diced
- 1/2 zucchini, diced
- 1/2 small onion, diced
- 1 tbsp olive oil
- 1/2 tsp turmeric
- 1/2 tsp paprika
- Salt and pepper to taste

DIRECTIONS

1. Heat olive oil in a skillet over medium heat.
2. Add the onion and bell pepper, and sauté for 5 minutes.
3. Add the zucchini and cook for another 3 minutes.
4. Stir in the crumbled tofu, turmeric, and paprika.
5. Cook until the tofu is heated through, about 5 minutes.
6. Season with salt and pepper.
7. Serve hot.

Ingredient Tips:

- Tofu: High in protein, low glycemic index, promotes satiety.
- Vegetables: Low glycemic index, high in vitamins and fiber.

Nutrient Content (per serving):

- Calories: 200
- Total Fat: 12g
- Protein: 14g
- Carbohydrates: 12g
- Sugars: 3g
- Fiber: 4g
- Sodium: 200mg

SPELT FLOUR SAVORY PANCAKES

Servings: 2 | Prep Time: 10 mins | Cook Time: 10 mins | Carbs per Serving: 30g

INGREDIENTS

- 1 cup spelt flour
- 1/2 cup milk (dairy or plant-based)
- 1 large egg
- 1/2 cup grated zucchini
- 1/4 cup chopped spinach
- 1/4 cup diced red onion
- 1 tbsp olive oil
- 1/2 tsp baking powder
- Salt and pepper to taste

DIRECTIONS

1. In a bowl, whisk together the spelt flour, baking powder, salt, and pepper.
2. In another bowl, mix the milk and egg.
3. Combine the wet and dry ingredients, then fold in the grated zucchini, chopped spinach, and diced red onion.
4. Heat olive oil in a skillet over medium heat.
5. Pour 1/4 cup of batter onto the skillet and cook until bubbles form on the surface, then flip and cook until golden brown, about 2-3 minutes per side.
6. Serve hot.

Ingredient Tips:

- Spelt Flour: Lower glycemic index than wheat, high in fiber.
- Vegetables: Low glycemic index, high in vitamins and fiber.

Nutrient Content (per serving):

- Calories: 250
- Total Fat: 10g
- Protein: 8g
- Carbohydrates: 30g
- Sugars: 3g
- Fiber: 5g
- Sodium: 200mg

KAMUT AND VEGETABLE STIR-FRY

Servings: 2 | Prep Time: 10 mins | Cook Time: 10 mins | Carbs per Serving: 40g

INGREDIENTS

- 1/2 cup cooked kamut
- 1/2 cup broccoli florets
- 1/2 bell pepper, sliced
- 1/2 carrot, julienned
- 1/2 cup snap peas
- 1 tbsp olive oil
- 1 tbsp soy sauce (low sodium)
- 1 clove garlic, minced
- 1/2 tsp ginger, minced

DIRECTIONS

1. Heat olive oil in a large skillet over medium heat.
2. Add the garlic and ginger, and sauté for 1 minute.
3. Add the broccoli, bell pepper, carrot, and snap peas, and cook for 5 minutes.
4. Stir in the cooked kamut and soy sauce.
5. Cook for another 3 minutes, until everything is heated through.
6. Serve hot.

Ingredient Tips:

- Kamut: Ancient grain with a low glycemic index, high in protein and fiber.
- Vegetables: Low glycemic index, high in vitamins and fiber.

Nutrient Content (per serving):

- Calories: 300
- Total Fat: 10g
- Protein: 12g
- Carbohydrates: 40g
- Sugars: 6g
- Fiber: 8g
- Sodium: 400mg

EGG AND VEGETABLE MUFFINS

Servings: 6 | Prep Time: 10 mins | Cook Time: 25 mins | Carbs per Serving: 3g

INGREDIENTS

- 6 large eggs
- 1/2 cup diced bell pepper
- 1/2 cup chopped spinach
- 1/4 cup diced red onion
- 1/4 cup feta cheese, crumbled (optional)
- Salt and pepper to taste
- 1 tbsp olive oil

DIRECTIONS

1. Preheat the oven to 350°F (175°C) and grease a muffin tin with olive oil.
2. In a bowl, whisk the eggs with salt and pepper.
3. Stir in the bell pepper, spinach, red onion, and feta cheese.
4. Pour the mixture into the muffin tin, filling each cup about 3/4 full.
5. Bake for 20-25 minutes, until the eggs are set.
6. Serve hot or store in the refrigerator for up to 3 days.

Ingredient Tips:

- Eggs: High in protein, helps stabilize blood sugar levels.
- Vegetables: Low glycemic index, high in vitamins and fiber.
- Feta Cheese: Adds flavor and protein, use in moderation.

Nutrient Content (per serving):

- Calories: 100
- Total Fat: 7g
- Protein: 8g
- Carbohydrates: 3g
- Sugars: 1g
- Fiber: 1g
- Sodium: 150mg

OATMEAL WITH SAVORY TOPPINGS

Servings: 1 | Prep Time: 5 mins | Cook Time: 10 mins | Carbs per Serving: 30g

INGREDIENTS

- 1/2 cup rolled oats
- 1 cup water
- 1/4 cup grated zucchini
- 1/4 cup diced cherry tomatoes
- 1 large egg
- 1 tbsp olive oil
- Salt and pepper to taste

DIRECTIONS

1. In a pot, cook the rolled oats with water according to package instructions.
2. In a skillet, heat olive oil over medium heat.
3. Add the grated zucchini and cherry tomatoes, and cook for 5 minutes.
4. Poach the egg in simmering water for 3-4 minutes.
5. Serve the oatmeal in a bowl, topped with the sautéed vegetables and poached egg.
6. Season with salt and pepper.

Ingredient Tips:

- Oats: Low glycemic index, high in fiber.
- Vegetables: Low glycemic index, high in vitamins and fiber.
- Egg: High in protein, helps stabilize blood sugar levels.

Nutrient Content (per serving):

- Calories: 300
- Total Fat: 14g
- Protein: 10g
- Carbohydrates: 30g
- Sugars: 4g
- Fiber: 6g
- Sodium: 200mg

BREAKFAST STUFFED BELL PEPPERS

Servings: 4 | Prep Time: 10 mins | Cook Time: 25 mins | Carbs per Serving: 25g

INGREDIENTS

- 2 large bell peppers, halved and seeded
- 1/2 cup cooked quinoa
- 1/4 cup black beans, rinsed and drained
- 1/4 cup corn kernels
- 1/4 cup diced tomatoes
- 1/4 cup shredded cheddar cheese (optional)
- 1 tbsp olive oil
- Salt and pepper to taste

DIRECTIONS

1. Preheat the oven to 375°F (190°C).
2. In a bowl, mix the cooked quinoa, black beans, corn, diced tomatoes, and olive oil. Season with salt and pepper.
3. Stuff the bell pepper halves with the quinoa mixture.
4. Place the stuffed peppers on a baking sheet and sprinkle with shredded cheddar cheese if using.
5. Bake for 20-25 minutes, until the peppers are tender and the filling is heated through.
6. Serve hot.

Ingredient Tips:

- Bell Peppers: Low glycemic index, high in vitamins and fiber.
- Quinoa: Low glycemic index, high in protein and fiber.
- Black Beans: High in fiber and protein, promotes steady glucose release.

Nutrient Content (per serving):

- Calories: 200
- Total Fat: 8g
- Protein: 8g
- Carbohydrates: 25g
- Sugars: 5g
- Fiber: 6g
- Sodium: 200mg

BAKED AVOCADO WITH EGG

Servings: 2 | Prep Time: 5 mins | Cook Time: 20 mins | Carbs per Serving: 12g

INGREDIENTS

- 1 large avocado, halved and pitted
- 2 large eggs
- Salt and pepper to taste
- 1 tbsp chopped chives (optional)

DIRECTIONS

1. Preheat the oven to 425°F (220°C).
2. Scoop out a bit of the avocado flesh to make room for the egg.
3. Place the avocado halves in a baking dish.
4. Crack an egg into each avocado half.
5. Season with salt and pepper.
6. Bake for 15-20 minutes, until the eggs are set.
7. Garnish with chopped chives if desired.
8. Serve hot.

Ingredient Tips:

- Avocado: High in healthy fats and fiber, promotes satiety.
- Eggs: High in protein, helps stabilize blood sugar levels.

Nutrient Content (per serving):

- Calories: 300
- Total Fat: 24g
- Protein: 12g
- Carbohydrates: 12g
- Sugars: 1g
- Fiber: 8g
- Sodium: 150mg

BROCCOLI AND CHEESE BREAKFAST CASSEROLE

Servings: 4 | Prep Time: 10 mins | Cook Time: 30 mins | Carbs per Serving: 8g

INGREDIENTS

- 2 cups broccoli florets
- 6 large eggs
- 1/2 cup milk (dairy or plant-based)
- 1 cup shredded cheddar cheese
- 1/2 cup diced red onion
- 1 tbsp olive oil
- Salt and pepper to taste

DIRECTIONS

1. Preheat the oven to 350°F (175°C) and grease a baking dish with olive oil.
2. In a skillet, heat olive oil over medium heat.
3. Add the diced red onion and sauté for 5 minutes.
4. In a bowl, whisk the eggs with milk, salt, and pepper.
5. Stir in the broccoli florets, sautéed onion, and shredded cheddar cheese.
6. Pour the mixture into the prepared baking dish.
7. Bake for 25-30 minutes, until the eggs are set.
8. Serve hot.

Ingredient Tips:

- Broccoli: Low glycemic index, high in vitamins and fiber.
- Eggs: High in protein, helps stabilize blood sugar levels.
- Cheddar Cheese: Adds flavor and protein, use in moderation.

Nutrient Content (per serving):

- Calories: 250
- Total Fat: 16g
- Protein: 16g
- Carbohydrates: 8g
- Sugars: 2g
- Fiber: 2g
- Sodium: 300mg

CAULIFLOWER BREAKFAST RICE

Servings: 2 | Prep Time: 10 mins | Cook Time: 10 mins | Carbs per Serving: 12g

INGREDIENTS

- 2 cups cauliflower rice
- 1/2 cup peas
- 1/2 cup diced carrots
- 1/2 small onion, diced
- 1 clove garlic, minced
- 1 tbsp olive oil
- 2 large eggs, beaten
- 1 tbsp soy sauce (low sodium)
- Salt and pepper to taste

DIRECTIONS

1. In a large skillet, heat olive oil over medium heat.
2. Add the onion, garlic, peas, and carrots, and cook for 5 minutes.
3. Add the cauliflower rice and cook for another 5 minutes.
4. Push the vegetables to the side of the skillet and pour the beaten eggs into the empty space.
5. Scramble the eggs until fully cooked, then mix them with the vegetables.
6. Stir in the soy sauce and season with salt and pepper.
7. Serve hot.

Ingredient Tips:

- Cauliflower: Low glycemic index, high in vitamins and fiber.
- Eggs: High in protein, helps stabilize blood sugar levels.
- Vegetables: Low glycemic index, high in vitamins and fiber.

Nutrient Content (per serving):

- Calories: 200
- Total Fat: 10g
- Protein: 10g
- Carbohydrates: 15g
- Sugars: 5g
- Fiber: 6g
- Sodium: 300mg

QUINOA BREAKFAST BOWL

Servings: 1 | Prep Time: 10 mins | Cook Time: 10 mins | Carbs per Serving: 30g

INGREDIENTS

- 1/2 cup cooked quinoa
- 1/2 cup diced cherry tomatoes
- 1/4 cup diced cucumber
- 1/4 cup diced avocado
- 1 large egg
- 1 tbsp olive oil
- Salt and pepper to taste
- 1 tbsp lemon juice

DIRECTIONS

1. Cook the quinoa according to package instructions.
2. In a bowl, mix the cooked quinoa with cherry tomatoes, cucumber, and avocado.
3. Poach the egg in simmering water for 3-4 minutes.
4. Top the quinoa mixture with the poached egg.
5. Drizzle with olive oil and lemon juice.
6. Season with salt and pepper.
7. Serve immediately.

Ingredient Tips:

- Quinoa: Low glycemic index, high in protein and fiber.
- Vegetables: Low glycemic index, high in vitamins and fiber.
- Egg: High in protein, helps stabilize blood sugar levels.
- Avocado: High in healthy fats and fiber, promotes satiety.

Nutrient Content (per serving):

- Calories: 300
- Total Fat: 14g
- Protein: 10g
- Carbohydrates: 30g
- Sugars: 5g
- Fiber: 8g
- Sodium: 150mg

MILLET PORRIDGE WITH SPINACH AND MUSHROOMS

Servings: 1 | Prep Time: 10 mins | Cook Time: 20 mins | Carbs per Serving: 40g

INGREDIENTS

- 1/2 cup millet
- 1 cup water
- 1 cup fresh spinach, chopped
- 1/2 cup sliced mushrooms
- 1 tbsp olive oil
- Salt and pepper to taste

DIRECTIONS

1. In a pot, cook the millet with water according to package instructions.
2. In a skillet, heat olive oil over medium heat.
3. Add the sliced mushrooms and cook for 5 minutes.
4. Add the chopped spinach and cook until wilted, about 2 minutes.
5. Stir the cooked millet into the skillet with the spinach and mushrooms.
6. Season with salt and pepper.
7. Serve hot.

Ingredient Tips:

- Millet: Low glycemic index, high in fiber and protein.
- Spinach: Low glycemic index, high in vitamins and fiber.
- Mushrooms: Low glycemic index, adds umami flavor.

Nutrient Content (per serving):

- Calories: 300
- Total Fat: 10g
- Protein: 10g
- Carbohydrates: 40g
- Sugars: 2g
- Fiber: 6g
- Sodium: 200mg

BUCKWHEAT BREAKFAST BOWL

Servings: 1 | Prep Time: 10 mins | Cook Time: 10 mins | Carbs per Serving: 30g

INGREDIENTS

- 1/2 cup cooked buckwheat
- 1/2 cup diced cherry tomatoes
- 1/4 cup diced cucumber
- 1/4 cup diced avocado
- 1 large egg
- 1 tbsp olive oil
- Salt and pepper to taste
- 1 tbsp lemon juice

DIRECTIONS

1. Cook the buckwheat according to package instructions.
2. In a bowl, mix the cooked buckwheat with cherry tomatoes, cucumber, and avocado.
3. Poach the egg in simmering water for 3-4 minutes.
4. Top the buckwheat mixture with the poached egg.
5. Drizzle with olive oil and lemon juice.
6. Season with salt and pepper.
7. Serve immediately.

Ingredient Tips:

- Buckwheat: Low glycemic index, high in protein and fiber.
- Vegetables: Low glycemic index, high in vitamins and fiber.
- Egg: High in protein, helps stabilize blood sugar levels.
- Avocado: High in healthy fats and fiber, promotes satiety.

Nutrient Content (per serving):

- Calories: 300
- Total Fat: 14g
- Protein: 10g
- Carbohydrates: 30g
- Sugars: 5g
- Fiber: 8g
- Sodium: 150mg

CHIA SEED PUDDING WITH ALMONDS AND BERRIES

Servings: 2 | Prep Time: 5 mins | Cook Time: none | Carbs per Serving: 20g

INGREDIENTS

- 1/4 cup chia seeds
- 1 cup almond milk
- 1 tbsp maple syrup (optional)
- 1/4 cup sliced almonds
- 1/4 cup mixed berries

DIRECTIONS

1. In a bowl, mix the chia seeds, almond milk, and maple syrup.
2. Refrigerate for at least 2 hours or overnight until the mixture thickens.
3. Top the chia seed pudding with sliced almonds and mixed berries.
4. Serve chilled.

Ingredient Tips:

- Chia Seeds: High in fiber and omega-3 fatty acids.
- Almond Milk: Low in calories and carbs, dairy-free option.
- Berries: Low glycemic index, high in antioxidants.

Nutrient Content (per serving):

- Calories: 200
- Total Fat: 12g
- Protein: 6g
- Carbohydrates: 20g
- Sugars: 10g
- Fiber: 10g
- Sodium: 100mg

SAVORY AMARANTH BREAKFAST PORRIDGE

Servings: 2 | Prep Time: 10 mins | Cook Time: 20 mins | Carbs per Serving: 35g

INGREDIENTS

- 1/2 cup amaranth
- 1 cup water
- 1/4 cup grated zucchini
- 1/4 cup diced tomatoes
- 1 clove garlic, minced
- 1 tbsp olive oil
- Salt and pepper to taste

DIRECTIONS

1. In a pot, cook the amaranth with water according to package instructions.
2. In a skillet, heat olive oil over medium heat.
3. Add the garlic, grated zucchini, and diced tomatoes, and cook for 5 minutes.
4. Stir the cooked amaranth into the skillet with the vegetables.
5. Season with salt and pepper.
6. Serve hot.

Ingredient Tips:

- Amaranth: Low glycemic index, high in protein and fiber.
- Vegetables: Low glycemic index, high in vitamins and fiber.

Nutrient Content (per serving):

- Calories: 250
- Total Fat: 10g
- Protein: 8g
- Carbohydrates: 35g
- Sugars: 4g
- Fiber: 8g
- Sodium: 150mg

SWEET POTATO AND BLACK BEAN BREAKFAST HASH

Servings: 2 | Prep Time: 10 mins | Cook Time: 20 mins | Carbs per Serving: 35g

INGREDIENTS

- 1 large sweet potato, diced
- 1/2 cup black beans, rinsed and drained
- 1/2 small onion, diced
- 1 bell pepper, diced
- 1 clove garlic, minced
- 1 tbsp olive oil
- 1/2 tsp cumin
- Salt and pepper to taste

DIRECTIONS

1. In a large skillet, heat olive oil over medium heat.
2. Add the diced sweet potato and cook for 10 minutes, stirring occasionally.
3. Add the onion, bell pepper, and garlic, and cook for another 5 minutes.
4. Stir in the black beans and cumin, and cook for another 3 minutes.
5. Season with salt and pepper.
6. Serve hot.

Ingredient Tips:

- Sweet Potato: Low glycemic index, high in fiber and vitamins.
- Black Beans: High in fiber and protein, promotes steady glucose release.
- Vegetables: Low glycemic index, high in vitamins and fiber.

Nutrient Content (per serving):

- Calories: 250
- Total Fat: 8g
- Protein: 8g
- Carbohydrates: 35g
- Sugars: 10g
- Fiber: 10g
- Sodium: 200mg

SPINACH AND TOFU SCRAMBLE

Servings: 2 | Prep Time: 10 mins | Cook Time: 10 mins | Carbs per Serving: 10g

INGREDIENTS

- 1 block firm tofu, crumbled
- 1 cup fresh spinach, chopped
- 1/2 small onion, diced
- 1 clove garlic, minced
- 1 tbsp olive oil
- 1/2 tsp turmeric
- Salt and pepper to taste

DIRECTIONS

1. In a large skillet, heat olive oil over medium heat.
2. Add the diced onion and garlic, and cook for 5 minutes.
3. Stir in the crumbled tofu and turmeric, and cook for another 5 minutes.
4. Add the chopped spinach and cook until wilted, about 2 minutes.
5. Season with salt and pepper.
6. Serve hot.

Ingredient Tips:

- Tofu: High in protein, low in carbs, plant-based.
- Spinach: Low glycemic index, high in vitamins and fiber.

Nutrient Content (per serving):

- Calories: 200
- Total Fat: 14g
- Protein: 16g
- Carbohydrates: 10g
- Sugars: 2g
- Fiber: 4g
- Sodium: 200mg

FARRO AND VEGETABLE BREAKFAST BOWL

Servings: 1 | Prep Time: 10 mins | Cook Time: 10 mins | Carbs per Serving: 35g

INGREDIENTS

- 1/2 cup cooked farro
- 1/2 cup diced cherry tomatoes
- 1/4 cup diced cucumber
- 1/4 cup diced bell pepper
- 1 large egg
- 1 tbsp olive oil
- Salt and pepper to taste
- 1 tbsp lemon juice

DIRECTIONS

1. Cook the farro according to package instructions.
2. In a bowl, mix the cooked farro with cherry tomatoes, cucumber, and bell pepper.
3. Poach the egg in simmering water for 3-4 minutes.
4. Top the farro mixture with the poached egg.
5. Drizzle with olive oil and lemon juice.
6. Season with salt and pepper.
7. Serve immediately.

Ingredient Tips:

- Sweet Potato: Low glycemic index, high in fiber and vitamins.
- Black Beans: High in fiber and protein, promotes steady glucose release.
- Vegetables: Low glycemic index, high in vitamins and fiber.

Nutrient Content (per serving):

- Calories: 300
- Total Fat: 14g
- Protein: 12g
- Carbohydrates: 35g
- Sugars: 5g
- Fiber: 8g
- Sodium: 150mg

Chapter Four

Diabetic Friendly Lunch Recipes

QUINOA AND BLACK BEAN SALAD

Servings: 4 | Prep Time: 15 mins | Cook Time: 15 mins | Carbs per Serving: 35g

INGREDIENTS

- 1 cup quinoa
- 1 can (15 oz) black beans, rinsed and drained
- 1 cup cherry tomatoes, halved
- 1 avocado, diced
- 1/2 red onion, finely chopped
- 1/4 cup fresh cilantro, chopped
- 2 tbsp olive oil
- 1 tbsp lime juice
- Salt and pepper to taste
- Optional: 1/2 cup corn kernels (fresh or frozen)

DIRECTIONS

1. Prepare Quinoa: Rinse quinoa under cold water. In a medium saucepan, bring 2 cups of water to a boil. Add quinoa, reduce heat to low, cover, and simmer for about 15 minutes or until the water is absorbed. Fluff with a fork and let it cool.
2. Mix Ingredients: In a large bowl, combine the cooked quinoa, black beans, cherry tomatoes, avocado, red onion, and cilantro.
3. Dress Salad: In a small bowl, whisk together olive oil, lime juice, salt, and pepper. Pour over the salad and toss gently to combine.
4. Serve: Serve immediately or refrigerate for up to 2 days

Ingredient Tips:

- Quinoa: A high-protein grain with a low glycemic index that helps keep blood sugar levels stable.
- Avocado: Contains healthy fats that enhance satiety and stabilize blood sugar.

Nutrient Content (per serving):

- Calories: 320
- Total Fat: 16g
- Protein: 9g
- Carbohydrates: 35g
- Sugars: 3g
- Fiber: 10g
- Sodium: 240mg

LENTIL AND VEGETABLE SOUP

Servings: 4 | Prep Time: 10 mins | Cook Time: 40 mins | Carbs per Serving: 30g

INGREDIENTS

- 1 cup green or brown lentils, rinsed
- 1 carrot, diced
- 1 celery stalk, diced
- 1 onion, chopped
- 2 cloves garlic, minced
- 1 zucchini, diced
- 1 can (14.5 oz) diced tomatoes, no added salt
- 4 cups low-sodium vegetable broth
- 1 tsp dried thyme
- 1 tsp dried basil
- 2 tbsp olive oil
- Salt and pepper to taste

DIRECTIONS

1. Sauté Vegetables: In a large pot, heat olive oil over medium heat. Add onion, carrot, and celery, and sauté until softened, about 5 minutes.
2. Add Garlic and Spices: Stir in garlic, thyme, and basil, and cook for another 1 minute.
3. Cook Soup: Add lentils, diced tomatoes, zucchini, and vegetable broth. Bring to a boil, then reduce heat and simmer for 30-40 minutes, until lentils are tender.
4. Season: Season with salt and pepper to taste. Serve hot.

Nutrient Content (per serving):

- Calories: 230
- Total Fat: 7g
- Protein: 12g
- Carbohydrates: 30g
- Sugars: 6g
- Fiber: 10g
- Sodium: 400mg

Ingredient Tips:

- Lentils: High in protein and fiber, they help to maintain stable blood sugar levels.
- Vegetables: Provide essential vitamins and minerals without spiking blood sugar.

SPELT BERRY AND VEGGIE BOWL

Servings: 4 | Prep Time: 15 mins | Cook Time: 45 mins | Carbs per Serving: 40g

INGREDIENTS

- 1 cup spelt berries
- 1 red bell pepper, chopped
- 1 yellow bell pepper, chopped
- 1 zucchini, chopped
- 1 red onion, chopped
- 2 tbsp olive oil
- 1 tbsp balsamic vinegar
- 1 avocado, sliced
- 1/4 cup feta cheese, crumbled (optional)
- Salt and pepper to taste

DIRECTIONS

1. Cook Spelt Berries: In a medium saucepan, bring 3 cups of water to a boil. Add spelt berries, reduce heat, cover, and simmer for about 40 minutes or until tender. Drain and set aside.
2. Roast Vegetables: Preheat oven to 400°F (200°C). On a baking sheet, toss bell peppers, zucchini, and red onion with olive oil, salt, and pepper. Roast for 20-25 minutes, until tender and slightly charred.
3. Assemble Bowl: In a large bowl, combine cooked spelt berries and roasted vegetables. Drizzle with balsamic vinegar and toss to combine. Top with avocado slices and feta cheese, if using.
4. Serve: Serve warm or at room temperature.

Ingredient Tips:

- Spelt Berries: An ancient grain with a low glycemic index, providing steady energy.
- Roasted Vegetables: Enhance flavor without adding sugars or unhealthy fats.

Nutrient Content (per serving):

- Calories: 350
- Total Fat: 15g
- Protein: 10g
- Carbohydrates: 40g
- Sugars: 5g
- Fiber: 10g
- Sodium: 200mg

CHICKPEA AND SPINACH STEW

Servings: 4 | Prep Time: 10 mins | Cook Time: 25 mins | Carbs per Serving: 35g

INGREDIENTS

- 2 cans (15 oz each) chickpeas, rinsed and drained
- 1 onion, chopped
- 2 cloves garlic, minced
- 1 can (14.5 oz) diced tomatoes, no added salt
- 4 cups fresh spinach
- 2 cups low-sodium vegetable broth
- 1 tsp ground cumin
- 1 tsp paprika
- 2 tbsp olive oil
- Salt and pepper to taste

DIRECTIONS

1. Sauté Onions and Garlic: In a large pot, heat olive oil over medium heat. Add onion and cook until translucent, about 5 minutes. Add garlic and cook for another minute.
2. Add Spices and Tomatoes: Stir in cumin, paprika, and diced tomatoes. Cook for 5 minutes, until tomatoes start to break down.
3. Cook Stew: Add chickpeas and vegetable broth. Bring to a boil, then reduce heat and simmer for 15 minutes.
4. Add Spinach: Stir in fresh spinach and cook until wilted, about 3 minutes. Season with salt and pepper to taste.
5. Serve: Serve hot.

Nutrient Content (per serving):

- Calories: 260
- Total Fat: 9g
- Protein: 12g
- Carbohydrates: 35g
- Sugars: 6g
- Fiber: 10g
- Sodium: 400mg

Ingredient Tips:

- Chickpeas: High in fiber and protein, they help stabilize blood sugar levels.
- Spinach: Low in calories and high in essential nutrients, adding volume and nutrition to the stew.

BROWN RICE AND VEGGIE STIR-FRY

Servings: 4 | Prep Time: 10 mins | Cook Time: 50 mins | Carbs per Serving: 45g

INGREDIENTS

- 1 cup spelt berries
- 1 red bell pepper, chopped
- 1 yellow bell pepper, chopped
- 1 zucchini, chopped
- 1 red onion, chopped
- 2 tbsp olive oil
- 1 tbsp balsamic vinegar
- 1 avocado, sliced
- 1/4 cup feta cheese, crumbled (optional)
- Salt and pepper to taste

DIRECTIONS

1. Cook Spelt Berries: In a medium saucepan, bring 3 cups of water to a boil. Add spelt berries, reduce heat, cover, and simmer for about 40 minutes or until tender. Drain and set aside.
2. Roast Vegetables: Preheat oven to 400°F (200°C). On a baking sheet, toss bell peppers, zucchini, and red onion with olive oil, salt, and pepper. Roast for 20-25 minutes, until tender and slightly charred.
3. Assemble Bowl: In a large bowl, combine cooked spelt berries and roasted vegetables. Drizzle with balsamic vinegar and toss to combine. Top with avocado slices and feta cheese, if using.
4. Serve: Serve warm or at room temperature.

Ingredient Tips:

- Brown Rice: A whole grain with a low glycemic index, providing steady energy.
- Vegetables: High in fiber and nutrients, supporting balanced blood sugar levels

Nutrient Content (per serving):

- Calories: 320
- Total Fat: 12g
- Protein: 8g
- Carbohydrates: 45g
- Sugars: 6g
- Fiber: 8g
- Sodium: 500mg

QUINOA STUFFED BELL PEPPERS

Servings: 4 | Prep Time: 20 mins | Cook Time: 35 mins | Carbs per Serving: 40g

INGREDIENTS

- 4 large bell peppers
- 1 cup quinoa
- 1 can (15 oz) black beans, rinsed and drained
- 1 cup corn kernels (fresh or frozen)
- 1 cup diced tomatoes
- 1/2 cup red onion, chopped
- 2 cloves garlic, minced
- 1 tsp cumin
- 1 tsp chili powder
- 2 tbsp olive oil
- 1/4 cup fresh cilantro, chopped
- Salt and pepper to taste

DIRECTIONS

1. Prepare Quinoa: Rinse quinoa under cold water. In a medium saucepan, bring 2 cups of water to a boil. Add quinoa, reduce heat to low, cover, and simmer for about 15 minutes or until the water is absorbed. Fluff with a fork and set aside.
2. Prepare Bell Peppers: Preheat oven to 375°F (190°C). Cut the tops off the bell peppers and remove the seeds and membranes. Place them in a baking dish.
3. Prepare Filling: In a large skillet, heat olive oil over medium heat. Add onion and garlic, and sauté until softened, about 5 minutes. Stir in black beans, corn, diced tomatoes, cumin, and chili powder. Cook for another 5 minutes. Add cooked quinoa and cilantro, and mix well. Season with salt and pepper to taste.
4. Stuff Peppers: Fill each bell pepper with the quinoa mixture. Cover the baking dish with foil and bake for 30-35 minutes, until peppers are tender.
5. Serve: Serve hot.

Ingredient Tips:

- Quinoa: Provides complete protein and a low glycemic index for steady energy.
- Bell Peppers: Rich in vitamins and antioxidants, low in calories

Nutrient Content (per serving):

- Calories: 280
- Total Fat: 9g
- Protein: 10g
- Carbohydrates: 40g
- Sugars: 8g
- Fiber: 10g
- Sodium: 300mg

SPINACH AND FETA STUFFED MUSHROOMS

Servings: 4 | Prep Time: 15 mins | Cook Time: 25 mins | Carbs per Serving: 25g

INGREDIENTS

- 4 large portobello mushrooms, stems removed
- 1 cup quinoa
- 2 cups fresh spinach, chopped
- 1/2 cup feta cheese, crumbled
- 1/4 cup sun-dried tomatoes, chopped
- 1 clove garlic, minced
- 2 tbsp olive oil
- 1 tbsp lemon juice
- Salt and pepper to taste

DIRECTIONS

1. Prepare Quinoa: Rinse quinoa under cold water. In a medium saucepan, bring 2 cups of water to a boil. Add quinoa, reduce heat to low, cover, and simmer for about 15 minutes or until the water is absorbed. Fluff with a fork and set aside.
2. Preheat Oven: Preheat oven to 375°F (190°C).
3. Prepare Filling: In a large skillet, heat olive oil over medium heat. Add garlic and cook for 1 minute. Stir in spinach and cook until wilted, about 3 minutes. Remove from heat and stir in cooked quinoa, feta cheese, sun-dried tomatoes, and lemon juice. Season with salt and pepper to taste.
4. Stuff Mushrooms: Place portobello mushrooms on a baking sheet. Fill each mushroom cap with the quinoa mixture.
5. Bake: Bake for 20-25 minutes, until mushrooms are tender.
6. Serve: Serve warm

Ingredient Tips:

- Quinoa: A complete protein with a low glycemic index, supporting stable blood sugar.
- Spinach: Provides essential nutrients and adds volume without many calories.

Nutrient Content (per serving):

- Calories: 250
- Total Fat: 11g
- Protein: 10g
- Carbohydrates: 25g
- Sugars: 4g
- Fiber: 5g
- Sodium: 350mg

MEDITERRANEAN CHICKPEA SALAD

Servings: 4 | Prep Time: 15 mins | Cook Time: 15 mins | Carbs per Serving: 20g

INGREDIENTS

- 1 can (15 oz) chickpeas, rinsed and drained
- 1 cucumber, diced
- 1 cup cherry tomatoes, halved
- 1/4 cup red onion, finely chopped
- 1/4 cup Kalamata olives, pitted and sliced
- 1/4 cup feta cheese, crumbled
- 2 tbsp olive oil
- 1 tbsp lemon juice
- 1 tsp dried oregano
- Salt and pepper to taste

DIRECTIONS

1. Prepare Salad: In a large bowl, combine chickpeas, cucumber, cherry tomatoes, red onion, olives, and feta cheese.
2. Make Dressing: In a small bowl, whisk together olive oil, lemon juice, oregano, salt, and pepper.
3. Toss Salad: Pour dressing over the salad and toss to combine.
4. Serve: Serve immediately or refrigerate for up to 2 days.

Ingredient Tips:

- Chickpeas: Provide fiber and protein, helping to maintain stable blood sugar.
- Olives and Olive Oil: Contain healthy fats that promote satiety and balanced blood sugar.

Nutrient Content (per serving):

- Calories: 200
- Total Fat: 11g
- Protein: 6g
- Carbohydrates: 20g
- Sugars: 4g
- Fiber: 5g
- Sodium: 300mg

BAKED SALMON WITH QUINOA AND ASPARAGUS

Servings: 4 | Prep Time: 15 mins | Cook Time: 20mins | Carbs per Serving: 25g

INGREDIENTS

- 4 salmon fillets (about 4 oz each)
- 1 cup quinoa
- 1 bunch asparagus, trimmed
- 2 tbsp olive oil
- 1 lemon, sliced
- 2 cloves garlic, minced
- Salt and pepper to taste

DIRECTIONS

1. Prepare Quinoa: Rinse quinoa under cold water. In a medium saucepan, bring 2 cups of water to a boil. Add quinoa, reduce heat to low, cover, and simmer for about 15 minutes or until the water is absorbed. Fluff with a fork and set aside.
2. Preheat Oven: Preheat oven to 375°F (190°C).
3. Prepare Asparagus: On a baking sheet, toss asparagus with 1 tbsp olive oil, salt, and pepper. Spread in a single layer.
4. Prepare Salmon: Place salmon fillets on a separate baking sheet. Drizzle with remaining olive oil, and sprinkle with garlic, salt, and pepper. Top each fillet with a lemon slice.
5. Bake: Bake asparagus and salmon for 15-20 minutes, until salmon is cooked through and asparagus is tender.
6. Serve: Serve salmon and asparagus over a bed of quinoa

Ingredient Tips:

- Salmon: Rich in omega-3 fatty acids, supporting heart health and balanced blood sugar.
- Quinoa: Provides complete protein and steady energy.

Nutrient Content (per serving):

- Calories: 350
- Total Fat: 16g
- Protein: 28g

- Calories: 350
- Total Fat: 16g
- Protein: 28g

BLACK BEAN AND AVOCADO WRAP

Servings: 4 | Prep Time: 15 mins | Cook Time: 0 mins | Carbs per Serving: 35g

INGREDIENTS

- 4 whole-grain tortillas
- 1 can (15 oz) black beans, rinsed and drained
- 1 avocado, sliced
- 1 cup shredded lettuce
- 1/2 cup cherry tomatoes, halved
- 1/4 cup red onion, thinly sliced
- 2 tbsp lime juice
- 2 tbsp olive oil
- 1/4 cup fresh cilantro, chopped
- Salt and pepper to taste

DIRECTIONS

1. Prepare Filling: In a large bowl, combine black beans, avocado, lettuce, cherry tomatoes, red onion, lime juice, olive oil, cilantro, salt, and pepper. Toss gently to combine.
2. Assemble Wraps: Lay out tortillas and evenly distribute the filling among them. Roll up each tortilla tightly.
3. Serve: Serve immediately or wrap in foil and refrigerate for up to 1 day.

Ingredient Tips:

- Black Beans: High in fiber and protein, supporting stable blood sugar levels.
- Avocado: Provides healthy fats that enhance satiety and blood sugar control.

Nutrient Content (per serving):

- Calories: 300
- Total Fat: 12g
- Protein: 9g

- Carbohydrates: 35g
- Sugars: 3g
- Fiber: 10g
- Sodium: 350mg

KALE & QUINOA SALAD WITH LEMON-TAHINI DRESSING

Servings: 4 | Prep Time: 15 mins | Cook Time: 15mins | Carbs per Serving: 30g

INGREDIENTS

- 1 bunch kale, stems removed and chopped
- 1 cup quinoa
- 1/2 cup shredded carrots
- 1/4 cup red cabbage, thinly sliced
- 1/4 cup pumpkin seeds
- 1/4 cup dried cranberries (unsweetened)
- 1/4 cup tahini
- 2 tbsp lemon juice
- 2 tbsp olive oil
- 1 clove garlic, minced
- 1 tbsp water (as needed)
- Salt and pepper to taste

DIRECTIONS

1. Prepare Quinoa: Rinse quinoa under cold water. In a medium saucepan, bring 2 cups of water to a boil. Add quinoa, reduce heat to low, cover, and simmer for about 15 minutes or until the water is absorbed. Fluff with a fork and set aside.
2. Prepare Dressing: In a small bowl, whisk together tahini, lemon juice, olive oil, garlic, salt, and pepper. Add water as needed to reach desired consistency.
3. Assemble Salad: In a large bowl, combine kale, quinoa, carrots, red cabbage, pumpkin seeds, and dried cranberries.
4. Toss Salad: Pour dressing over the salad and toss to combine.
5. Serve: Serve immediately or refrigerate for up to 2 days

Ingredient Tips:

- Kale: High in fiber and nutrients, supporting balanced blood sugar levels.
- Tahini: Provides healthy fats and a creamy texture to the dressing.

Nutrient Content (per serving):

- Calories: 290
- Total Fat: 14g
- Protein: 9g
- Carbohydrates: 30g
- Sugars: 5g
- Fiber: 7g
- Sodium: 220mg

SPELT AND LENTIL PILAF

Servings: 4 | Prep Time: 15 mins | Cook Time: 45 mins | Carbs per Serving: 35g

INGREDIENTS

- 1 cup spelt berries
- 1 cup green lentils, rinsed
- 1 onion, chopped
- 2 cloves garlic, minced
- 1 carrot, diced
- 2 celery stalks, diced
- 4 cups low-sodium vegetable broth
- 2 tbsp olive oil
- 1 tsp dried thyme
- 1/4 cup fresh parsley, chopped
- Salt and pepper to taste

DIRECTIONS

1. Prepare Spelt Berries: In a medium saucepan, bring 3 cups of water to a boil. Add spelt berries, reduce heat, cover, and simmer for about 40 minutes or until tender. Drain and set aside.
2. Sauté Vegetables: In a large pot, heat olive oil over medium heat. Add onion, carrot, and celery, and sauté until softened, about 5 minutes. Add garlic and thyme, and cook for another minute.
3. Cook Pilaf: Add lentils and vegetable broth. Bring to a boil, then reduce heat and simmer for 20-25 minutes, until lentils are tender.
4. Combine: Stir in cooked spelt berries and parsley. Season with salt and pepper to taste.
5. Serve: Serve hot

Ingredient Tips:

- Spelt: An ancient grain with a low glycemic index, providing steady energy.
- Lentils: High in protein and fiber, helping to maintain stable blood sugar levels

Nutrient Content (per serving):

- Calories: 280
- Total Fat: 8g
- Protein: 12g
- Carbohydrates: 35g
- Sugars: 4g
- Fiber: 8g
- Sodium: 350mg

AVOCADO AND CHICKPEA STUFFED SWEET POTATOES

Servings: 4 | Prep Time: 15 mins | Cook Time: 50mins | Carbs per Serving: 40g

INGREDIENTS

- 4 medium sweet potatoes
- 1 can (15 oz) chickpeas, rinsed and drained
- 1 avocado, diced
- 1/4 cup red onion, finely chopped
- 1/4 cup fresh cilantro, chopped
- 1 tbsp lime juice
- 2 tbsp olive oil
- Salt and pepper to taste

DIRECTIONS

1. Bake Sweet Potatoes: Preheat oven to 400°F (200°C). Pierce sweet potatoes with a fork and bake for 45-50 minutes, until tender.
2. Prepare Filling: In a large bowl, combine chickpeas, avocado, red onion, cilantro, lime juice, olive oil, salt, and pepper. Toss gently to combine.
3. Stuff Sweet Potatoes: Cut sweet potatoes open lengthwise and fluff the insides with a fork. Fill each sweet potato with the chickpea and avocado mixture.
4. Serve: Serve warm.

Ingredient Tips:

- Sweet Potatoes: Rich in fiber and vitamins, they have a moderate glycemic index.
- Avocado and Chickpeas: Provide healthy fats and protein, supporting balanced blood sugar.

Nutrient Content (per serving):

- Calories: 320
- Total Fat: 14g
- Protein: 6g
- Carbohydrates: 40g
- Sugars: 10g
- Fiber: 9g
- Sodium: 250mg

BROWN RICE AND VEGGIE SUSHI ROLLS

Servings: 4 | Prep Time: 20 mins | Cook Time: 40 mins | Carbs per Serving: 35g

INGREDIENTS

- 1 cup brown rice
- 1 tbsp rice vinegar
- 4 nori seaweed sheets
- 1 cucumber, julienned
- 1 carrot, julienned
- 1 avocado, sliced
- 1/4 cup red bell pepper, julienned
- 1 tbsp sesame seeds
- Low-sodium soy sauce for serving

DIRECTIONS

1. Prepare Brown Rice: Cook brown rice according to package instructions. Once cooked, stir in rice vinegar and let cool to room temperature.
2. Assemble Sushi: Lay out a nori sheet on a bamboo sushi mat. Spread an even layer of brown rice over the nori, leaving a 1-inch border at the top. Arrange cucumber, carrot, avocado, and red bell pepper in a line across the center of the rice.
3. Roll Sushi: Using the bamboo mat, roll the nori tightly around the filling. Moisten the top border with water to seal the roll. Repeat with remaining ingredients.
4. Slice and Serve: Slice each roll into 8 pieces. Sprinkle with sesame seeds and serve with low-sodium soy sauce.

Ingredient Tips:

- Brown Rice: A whole grain with a low glycemic index, providing steady energy.
- Vegetables: High in fiber and nutrients, supporting overall health and stable blood sugar levels

Nutrient Content (per serving):

- Calories: 250
- Total Fat: 8g
- Protein: 5g
- Carbohydrates: 35g
- Sugars: 3g
- Fiber: 6g
- Sodium: 200mg

GREEK YOGURT PARFAIT WITH BERRIES AND NUTS

Servings: 4 | Prep Time: 10 mins | Cook Time: 0 mins | Carbs per Serving: 15g

INGREDIENTS

- 2 cups Greek yogurt
- 1 cup mixed berries (strawberries, blueberries, raspberries)
- 1/4 cup nuts (almonds, walnuts, or pecans), chopped
- 1 tbsp honey (optional)

DIRECTIONS

1. Assemble Parfaits: In four serving glasses, layer Greek yogurt, berries, and nuts. Drizzle with honey if desired.
2. Serve: Serve immediately.

Ingredient Tips:

- Greek Yogurt: High in protein, supporting muscle repair and satiety.
- Berries and Nuts: Provide fiber, antioxidants, and healthy fats, supporting balanced blood sugar.

Nutrient Content (per serving):

- Calories: 200
- Total Fat: 10g
- Protein: 12g
- Carbohydrates: 15g
- Sugars: 10g
- Fiber: 3g
- Sodium: 60mg

ROASTED VEGGIE AND HUMMUS BOWL

Servings: 4 | Prep Time: 15 mins | Cook Time: 25 mins | Carbs per Serving: 40g

INGREDIENTS

- 1 cup quinoa
- 1 red bell pepper, sliced
- 1 zucchini, sliced
- 1 red onion, sliced
- 1 cup cherry tomatoes
- 2 tbsp olive oil
- 1 tsp dried oregano
- Salt and pepper to taste
- 1 cup hummus
- 1/4 cup fresh parsley, chopped

DIRECTIONS

1. Prepare Quinoa: Rinse quinoa under cold water. In a medium saucepan, bring 2 cups of water to a boil. Add quinoa, reduce heat to low, cover, and simmer for about 15 minutes or until the water is absorbed. Fluff with a fork and set aside.
2. Preheat Oven: Preheat oven to 400°F (200°C).
3. Roast Vegetables: On a baking sheet, toss bell pepper, zucchini, red onion, and cherry tomatoes with olive oil, oregano, salt, and pepper. Roast for 20-25 minutes, until vegetables are tender.
4. Assemble Bowls: Divide cooked quinoa into four bowls. Top with roasted vegetables and a dollop of hummus. Sprinkle with fresh parsley.
5. Serve: Serve warm.

Ingredient Tips:

- Quinoa: Provides complete protein and has a low glycemic index.
- Hummus: Made from chickpeas, it offers fiber and protein, supporting stable blood sugar.

Nutrient Content (per serving):

- Calories: 350
- Total Fat: 15g
- Protein: 10g
- Carbohydrates: 40g
- Sugars: 8g
- Fiber: 10g
- Sodium: 300mg

GREEK YOGURT PARFAIT WITH BERRIES AND NUTS

Servings: 4 | Prep Time: 10 mins | Cook Time: 0mins | Carbs per Serving: 15g

INGREDIENTS

- 2 cups Greek yogurt
- 1 cup mixed berries (strawberries, blueberries, raspberries)
- 1/4 cup nuts (almonds, walnuts, or pecans), chopped
- 1 tbsp honey (optional)

DIRECTIONS

1. Assemble Parfaits: In four serving glasses, layer Greek yogurt, berries, and nuts. Drizzle with honey if desired.
2. Serve: Serve immediately.

Ingredient Tips:

- Greek Yogurt: High in protein, supporting muscle repair and satiety.
- Berries and Nuts: Provide fiber, antioxidants, and healthy fats, supporting balanced blood sugar.

Nutrient Content (per serving):

- Calories: 200
- Total Fat: 10g
- Protein: 12g
- Carbohydrates: 15g
- Sugars: 10g
- Fiber: 3g
- Sodium: 60mg

ROASTED VEGGIE AND HUMMUS BOWL

Servings: 4 | Prep Time: 15 mins | Cook Time: 25 mins | Carbs per Serving: 40g

INGREDIENTS

- 1 cup quinoa
- 1 red bell pepper, sliced
- 1 zucchini, sliced
- 1 red onion, sliced
- 1 cup cherry tomatoes
- 2 tbsp olive oil
- 1 tsp dried oregano
- Salt and pepper to taste
- 1 cup hummus
- 1/4 cup fresh parsley, chopped

DIRECTIONS

1. Prepare Quinoa: Rinse quinoa under cold water. In a medium saucepan, bring 2 cups of water to a boil. Add quinoa, reduce heat to low, cover, and simmer for about 15 minutes or until the water is absorbed. Fluff with a fork and set aside.
2. Preheat Oven: Preheat oven to 400°F (200°C).
3. Roast Vegetables: On a baking sheet, toss bell pepper, zucchini, red onion, and cherry tomatoes with olive oil, oregano, salt, and pepper. Roast for 20-25 minutes, until vegetables are tender.
4. Assemble Bowls: Divide cooked quinoa into four bowls. Top with roasted vegetables and a dollop of hummus. Sprinkle with fresh parsley.
5. Serve: Serve warm.

Ingredient Tips:

- Quinoa: Provides complete protein and has a low glycemic index.
- Hummus: Made from chickpeas, it offers fiber and protein, supporting stable blood sugar.

Nutrient Content (per serving):

- Calories: 350
- Total Fat: 15g
- Protein: 10g
- Carbohydrates: 40g
- Sugars: 8g
- Fiber: 10g
- Sodium: 300mg

CURRIED CHICKPEA AND SPINACH STEW

Servings: 4 | Prep Time: 10 mins | Cook Time: 40 mins | Carbs per Serving: 25g

INGREDIENTS

- 1 can (15 oz) chickpeas, rinsed and drained
- 1 onion, chopped
- 2 cloves garlic, minced
- 1 tbsp ginger, minced
- 1 tbsp curry powder
- 1 tsp ground cumin
- 1 can (14.5 oz) diced tomatoes
- 1 cup vegetable broth
- 4 cups fresh spinach
- 2 tbsp olive oil
- Salt and pepper to taste
- 1/4 cup fresh cilantro, chopped

DIRECTIONS

1. Sauté Aromatics: In a large pot, heat olive oil over medium heat. Add onion, garlic, and ginger, and sauté until softened, about 5 minutes. Stir in curry powder and cumin, and cook for another minute.
2. Add Chickpeas and Tomatoes: Add chickpeas, diced tomatoes, and vegetable broth. Bring to a boil, then reduce heat and simmer for 20 minutes.
3. Add Spinach: Stir in fresh spinach and cook until wilted, about 2-3 minutes. Season with salt and pepper to taste.
4. Serve: Serve hot, garnished with fresh cilantro.

Ingredient Tips:

- Chickpeas: High in fiber and protein, supporting stable blood sugar.
- Spinach: Packed with nutrients and adds volume to the stew without many calories

Nutrient Content (per serving):

- Calories: 220
- Total Fat: 8g
- Protein: 8g
- Carbohydrates: 25g
- Sugars: 7g
- Fiber: 8g
- Sodium: 400mg

QUINOA AND BLACK BEAN STUFFED TOMATOES

Servings: 4 | Prep Time: 20 mins | Cook Time: 15 mins | Carbs per Serving: 30g

INGREDIENTS

- 4 large tomatoes
- 1 cup quinoa
- 1 can (15 oz) black beans, rinsed and drained
- 1/2 cup corn kernels
- 1/4 cup red onion, finely chopped
- 1/4 cup fresh cilantro, chopped
- 1 tsp cumin
- 1 tsp chili powder
- 2 tbsp lime juice
- 2 tbsp olive oil
- Salt and pepper to taste

DIRECTIONS

1. Prepare Quinoa: Rinse quinoa under cold water. In a medium saucepan, bring 2 cups of water to a boil. Add quinoa, reduce heat to low, cover, and simmer for about 15 minutes or until the water is absorbed. Fluff with a fork and set aside.
2. Hollow Tomatoes: Cut the tops off the tomatoes and scoop out the insides. Set aside.
3. Mix Filling: In a large bowl, combine cooked quinoa, black beans, corn, red onion, cilantro, cumin, chili powder, lime juice, olive oil, salt, and pepper.
4. Stuff Tomatoes: Fill each tomato with the quinoa mixture.
5. Serve: Serve immediately, or chill for 30 minutes for a cold dish

Ingredient Tips:

- Quinoa: Provides complete protein and a low glycemic index for steady energy.
- Bell Peppers: Rich in vitamins and antioxidants, low in calories

Nutrient Content (per serving):

- Calories: 250
- Total Fat: 10g
- Protein: 8g
- Carbohydrates: 30g
- Sugars: 6g
- Fiber: 8g
- Sodium: 200mg

Chapter Five

Diabetic Friendly Salad Recipes

QUINOA AND BLACK BEAN SALAD

Servings: 4 | Prep Time: 15 mins | Cook Time: 0mins | Carbs per Serving: 32g

INGREDIENTS

- 1 cup cooked quinoa
- 1 cup black beans, drained and rinsed
- 1 red bell pepper, diced
- 1 small red onion, finely chopped
- 1 cup cherry tomatoes, halved
- 1 avocado, diced
- 1/4 cup fresh cilantro, chopped
- 2 tbsp olive oil
- 2 tbsp lime juice
- Salt and pepper to tast

DIRECTIONS

1. In a large bowl, combine cooked quinoa, black beans, bell pepper, red onion, cherry tomatoes, avocado, and cilantro.
2. In a small bowl, whisk together olive oil, lime juice, salt, and pepper.
3. Pour the dressing over the salad and toss to combine.
4. Serve immediately or refrigerate for later.

Ingredient Tips:

- Quinoa: Low glycemic index, high in protein and fiber.
- Black Beans: High in fiber and protein, promotes steady glucose release.

Nutrient Content (per serving):

- Calories: 300
- Total Fat: 14g
- Protein: 8g
- Carbohydrates: 32g
- Sugars: 3g
- Fiber: 10g
- Sodium: 150mg

SPINACH AND CHICKPEA SALAD

Servings: 2 | Prep Time: 10 mins | Cook Time:0 mins | Carbs per Serving: 28g

INGREDIENTS

- 4 cups fresh spinach leaves
- 1 can chickpeas, drained and rinsed
- 1/2 cup cucumber, diced
- 1/2 cup cherry tomatoes, halved
- 1/4 cup red onion, thinly sliced
- 2 tbsp olive oil
- 1 tbsp balsamic vinegar
- Salt and pepper to taste

DIRECTIONS

1. In a large bowl, combine spinach, chickpeas, cucumber, cherry tomatoes, and red onion.
2. In a small bowl, whisk together olive oil, balsamic vinegar, salt, and pepper.
3. Pour the dressing over the salad and toss to combine.
4. Serve immediately.

Ingredient Tips:

- Spinach: Low glycemic index, high in vitamins and fiber.
- Chickpeas: High in protein and fiber, helps manage blood sugar levels.

Nutrient Content (per serving):

- Calories: 250
- Total Fat: 12g
- Protein: 8g
- Carbohydrates: 28g
- Sugars: 4g
- Fiber: 8g
- Sodium: 200mg

LENTIL AND VEGETABLE SALAD

Servings: 4 | Prep Time: 15 mins | Cook Time: 0mins | Carbs per Serving: 25g

INGREDIENTS
- 1 cup cooked lentils
- 1/2 cup diced carrots
- 1/2 cup diced celery
- 1/2 cup diced cucumber
- 1/2 cup cherry tomatoes, halved
- 1/4 cup chopped parsley
- 2 tbsp olive oil
- 1 tbsp lemon juice
- Salt and pepper to taste

DIRECTIONS
1. In a large bowl, combine cooked lentils, carrots, celery, cucumber, cherry tomatoes, and parsley.
2. In a small bowl, whisk together olive oil, lemon juice, salt, and pepper.
3. Pour the dressing over the salad and toss to combine.
4. Serve immediately or refrigerate for later.

Ingredient Tips:
- Lentils: Low glycemic index, high in protein and fiber.
- Vegetables: Low glycemic index, high in vitamins and fiber.

Nutrient Content (per serving):
- Calories: 220
- Total Fat: 10g
- Protein: 8g
- Carbohydrates: 25g
- Sugars: 5g
- Fiber: 9g
- Sodium: 180mg

AVOCADO AND KALE SALAD

Servings: 2 | Prep Time: 10 mins | Cook Time: 0 mins | Carbs per Serving: 20g

INGREDIENTS
- 4 cups kale, chopped
- 1 avocado, diced
- 1/2 cup cherry tomatoes, halved
- 1/4 cup red onion, thinly sliced
- 2 tbsp olive oil
- 1 tbsp apple cider vinegar
- Salt and pepper to taste

DIRECTIONS
1. In a large bowl, combine kale, avocado, cherry tomatoes, and red onion.
2. In a small bowl, whisk together olive oil, apple cider vinegar, salt, and pepper.
3. Pour the dressing over the salad and toss to combine.
4. Serve immediately.

Ingredient Tips:
- Kale: High in fiber and vitamins, low glycemic index.
- Avocado: Provides healthy fats that enhance satiety and stabilize blood sugar levels.

Nutrient Content (per serving):
- Calories: 280
- Total Fat: 22g
- Protein: 4g
- Carbohydrates: 20g
- Sugars: 3g
- Fiber: 8g
- Sodium: 150mg

GREEK YOGURT AND CUCUMBER SALAD

Servings: 4 | Prep Time: 10 mins | Cook Time: 0mins | Carbs per Serving: 10g

INGREDIENTS

- 1 cup Greek yogurt (5% fat)
- 1 cucumber, diced
- 1/4 cup red onion, finely chopped
- 1 clove garlic, minced
- 1 tbsp fresh dill, chopped
- 1 tbsp lemon juice
- Salt and pepper to taste

DIRECTIONS

1. In a large bowl, combine the Greek yogurt, cucumber, red onion, garlic, dill, lemon juice, salt, and pepper.
2. Mix well until all ingredients are evenly coated.
3. Serve immediately or refrigerate for later.

Ingredient Tips:

- Greek Yogurt: High in protein, helps stabilize blood sugar levels.
- Cucumber: Low glycemic index, high in fiber and water content.

Nutrient Content (per serving):

- Calories: 150
- Total Fat: 8g
- Protein: 10g
- Carbohydrates: 10g
- Sugars: 6g
- Fiber: 2g
- Sodium: 200mg

BROWN RICE AND EDAMAME SALAD

Servings: 4 | Prep Time: 15 mins | Cook Time: 30 mins | Carbs per Serving: 40g

INGREDIENTS

- 1 cup brown rice, cooked
- 1 cup edamame, shelled and cooked
- 1/2 cup red bell pepper, diced
- 1/4 cup green onions, chopped
- 2 tbsp soy sauce (low sodium)
- 1 tbsp sesame oil
- 1 tbsp rice vinegar
- 1 tbsp sesame seeds

DIRECTIONS

1. Cook the brown rice according to package instructions and let it cool.
2. In a large bowl, combine the cooked brown rice, edamame, red bell pepper, and green onions.
3. In a small bowl, whisk together the soy sauce, sesame oil, and rice vinegar.
4. Pour the dressing over the salad and toss to combine.
5. Sprinkle with sesame seeds before serving.
6. Serve immediately or refrigerate for later.

Ingredient Tips:

- Brown Rice: Whole grain with a low glycemic index, high in fiber.
- Edamame: Provides protein and fiber for a steady release of glucose.
- Sesame Oil: Adds healthy fats that enhance satiety.

Nutrient Content (per serving):

- Calories: 300
- Total Fat: 10g
- Protein: 12g
- Carbohydrates: 40g
- Sugars: 3g
- Fiber: 6g
- Sodium: 250mg

SPELT AND AVOCADO SALAD

Servings: 4 | Prep Time: 15 mins | Cook Time: 30mins | Carbs per Serving: 35g

INGREDIENTS

- 1 cup spelt, cooked
- 1 avocado, diced
- 1 cup cherry tomatoes, halved
- 1/4 cup red onion, finely chopped
- 1/4 cup fresh basil, chopped
- 2 tbsp olive oil
- 1 tbsp lemon juice
- Salt and pepper to taste

DIRECTIONS

1. Cook the spelt according to package instructions and let it cool.
2. In a large bowl, combine the cooked spelt, avocado, cherry tomatoes, red onion, and basil.
3. In a small bowl, whisk together the olive oil, lemon juice, salt, and pepper.
4. Pour the dressing over the salad and toss to combine.
5. Serve immediately or refrigerate for later.

Ingredient Tips:

- Spelt: Ancient grain with a low glycemic index, high in fiber.
- Avocado: Provides healthy fats that enhance satiety and stabilize blood sugar levels.

Nutrient Content (per serving):

- Calories: 280
- Total Fat: 14g
- Protein: 8g
- Carbohydrates: 35g
- Sugars: 3g
- Fiber: 10g
- Sodium: 150mg

ROASTED BEET AND LENTIL SALAD

Servings: 4 | Prep Time: 15 mins | Cook Time: 45 mins | Carbs per Serving: 35g

INGREDIENTS

- 1 cup lentils, cooked
- 2 large beets, roasted and diced
- 1/4 cup red onion, thinly sliced
- 1/4 cup feta cheese, crumbled
- 2 tbsp olive oil
- 1 tbsp balsamic vinegar
- Salt and pepper to taste

DIRECTIONS

1. Preheat the oven to 400°F (200°C).
2. Wrap the beets in foil and roast for 45 minutes, or until tender. Let them cool, then peel and dice.
3. In a large bowl, combine the cooked lentils, roasted beets, red onion, and feta cheese.
4. In a small bowl, whisk together the olive oil, balsamic vinegar, salt, and pepper.
5. Pour the dressing over the salad and toss to combine.
6. Serve warm or chilled.

Ingredient Tips:

- Beets: Low glycemic index, high in fiber and vitamins.
- Lentils: High in protein and fiber, promoting a steady release of glucose.
- Feta Cheese: Adds a rich source of protein and healthy fats.

Nutrient Content (per serving):

- Calories: 250
- Total Fat: 10g
- Protein: 12g
- Carbohydrates: 35g
- Sugars: 10g
- Fiber: 10g
- Sodium: 200mg

MEDITERRANEAN CHICKPEA SALAD

Servings: 4 | Prep Time: 15 mins | Cook Time: 0mins | Carbs per Serving: 25g

INGREDIENTS

- 1 can chickpeas, rinsed and drained
- 1 cup cherry tomatoes, halved
- 1 cucumber, diced
- 1/4 cup red onion, finely chopped
- 1/4 cup Kalamata olives, pitted and sliced
- 1/4 cup feta cheese, crumbled
- 2 tbsp olive oil
- 1 tbsp red wine vinegar
- 1 tsp dried oregano
- Salt and pepper to taste

DIRECTIONS

1. In a large bowl, combine the chickpeas, cherry tomatoes, cucumber, red onion, olives, and feta cheese.
2. In a small bowl, whisk together the olive oil, red wine vinegar, oregano, salt, and pepper.
3. Pour the dressing over the salad and toss to combine.
4. Serve immediately or refrigerate for later.

Ingredient Tips:

- Chickpeas: Provide protein and fiber for a steady release of glucose.
- Olives: Add healthy fats that enhance satiety and flavor.
- Cucumber: Low glycemic index and high in water content.

Nutrient Content (per serving):

- Calories: 220
- Total Fat: 12g
- Protein: 8g
- Carbohydrates: 25g
- Sugars: 4g
- Fiber: 7g
- Sodium: 300mg

FARRO AND ARUGULA SALAD

Servings: 4 | Prep Time: 15 mins | Cook Time: 30 mins | Carbs per Serving: 35g

INGREDIENTS

- 1 cup farro, cooked
- 4 cups arugula, washed and chopped
- 1/2 cup cherry tomatoes, halved
- 1/4 cup red onion, thinly sliced
- 1/4 cup walnuts, chopped
- 2 tbsp olive oil
- 1 tbsp lemon juice
- Salt and pepper to taste

DIRECTIONS

1. Cook the farro according to package instructions and let it cool.
2. In a large bowl, combine the cooked farro, arugula, cherry tomatoes, red onion, and walnuts.
3. In a small bowl, whisk together the olive oil, lemon juice, salt, and pepper.
4. Pour the dressing over the salad and toss to combine.
5. Serve immediately or refrigerate for later.

Ingredient Tips:

- Farro: Ancient grain with a low glycemic index, high in fiber.
- Arugula: Low glycemic index, high in vitamins and fiber.
- Walnuts: Add healthy fats and enhance the salad's nutritional value.

Nutrient Content (per serving):

- Calories: 300
- Total Fat: 14g
- Protein: 10
- Carbohydrates: 35g
- Sugars: 3g
- Fiber: 8g
- Sodium: 150mg

Chapter Six

Diabetic Friendly Soup Recipes

LENTIL AND SPINACH SOUP

Servings: 4 | Prep Time: 15 mins | Cook Time: 40mins | Carbs per Serving: 30g

INGREDIENTS

- 1 cup lentils, rinsed
- 6 cups vegetable broth
- 1 onion, chopped
- 2 garlic cloves, minced
- 2 carrots, chopped
- 2 celery stalks, chopped
- 2 cups fresh spinach, chopped
- 2 tbsp olive oil
- 1 tsp cumin
- 1 tsp paprika
- Salt and pepper to taste

DIRECTIONS

1. In a large pot, heat the olive oil over medium heat Add the onion, garlic, carrots, and celery, and sauté until softened, about 5 minutes.
2. Add the cumin and paprika, and cook for another minute.
3. Stir in the lentils and vegetable broth. Bring to a boil, then reduce the heat and simmer for 25-30 minutes, or until the lentils are tender.
4. Add the spinach and cook for another 5 minutes.
5. Season with salt and pepper to taste. Serve warm.

Ingredient Tips:

- Lentils: High in protein and fiber, promoting a steady release of glucose.
- Spinach: Low glycemic index, high in vitamins and fiber.
- Olive Oil: Provides healthy fats that enhance satiety.

Nutrient Content (per serving):

- Calories: 200
- Total Fat: 8g
- Protein: 10g
- Carbohydrates: 30g
- Sugars: 4g
- Fiber: 10g
- Sodium: 400mg

QUINOA AND VEGETABLE SOUP

Servings: 4 | Prep Time: 15 mins | Cook Time: 35 mins | Carbs per Serving: 35g

INGREDIENTS

- 1 cup quinoa, rinsed
- 6 cups vegetable broth
- 1 onion, chopped
- 2 garlic cloves, minced
- 2 carrots, chopped
- 2 celery stalks, chopped
- 1 zucchini, chopped
- 1 cup cherry tomatoes, halved
- 2 tbsp olive oil
- 1 tsp thyme
- 1 tsp oregano
- Salt and pepper to taste

DIRECTIONS

1. In a large pot, heat the olive oil over medium heat. Add the onion, garlic, carrots, and celery, and sauté until softened, about 5 minutes.
2. Add the thyme and oregano, and cook for another minute.
3. Stir in the quinoa and vegetable broth. Bring to a boil, then reduce the heat and simmer for 20 minutes.
4. Add the zucchini and cherry tomatoes, and cook for another 10 minutes.
5. Season with salt and pepper to taste. Serve warm.

Ingredient Tips:

- Quinoa: High in protein and fiber, with a low glycemic index.
- Zucchini: Low glycemic index, high in vitamins and fiber.
- Olive Oil: Adds healthy fats that enhance satiety.

Nutrient Content (per serving):

- Calories: 250
- Total Fat: 10g
- Protein: 8g
- Carbohydrates: 35g
- Sugars: 6g
- Fiber: 8g
- Sodium: 450mg

CHICKEN AND VEGETABLE SOUP

Servings: 4 | Prep Time: 15 mins | Cook Time: 30mins | Carbs per Serving: 12g

INGREDIENTS

- 1 lb chicken breast, diced
- 6 cups chicken broth
- 1 onion, chopped
- 2 garlic cloves, minced
- 2 carrots, chopped
- 2 celery stalks, chopped
- 1 cup kale, chopped
- 2 tbsp olive oil
- 1 tsp thyme
- 1 tsp rosemary
- Salt and pepper to taste

DIRECTIONS

1. In a large pot, heat the olive oil over medium heat Add the onion, garlic, carrots, and celery, and sauté until softened, about 5 minutes.
2. Add the thyme and rosemary, and cook for another minute.
3. Stir in the chicken and chicken broth. Bring to a boil, then reduce the heat and simmer for 20 minutes, or until the chicken is cooked through.
4. Add the kale and cook for another 5 minutes.
5. Season with salt and pepper to taste. Serve warm.

Ingredient Tips:

- Chicken Breast: High in protein, essential for maintaining steady energy levels.
- Kale: Low glycemic index, high in fiber and vitamins.
- Olive Oil: Provides healthy fats that enhance satiety.

Nutrient Content (per serving):

- Calories: 210
- Total Fat: 10g
- Protein: 25g
- Carbohydrates: 12g
- Sugars: 4g
- Fiber: 4g
- Sodium: 500mg

BUTTERNUT SQUASH AND RED LENTIL SOUP

Servings: 4 | Prep Time: 15 mins | Cook Time: 25 mins | Carbs per Serving: 40g

INGREDIENTS

- 1 butternut squash, peeled and diced
- 1 cup red lentils, rinsed
- 6 cups vegetable broth
- 1 onion, chopped
- 2 garlic cloves, minced
- 1 tsp cumin
- 1 tsp turmeric
- 2 tbsp olive oil
- Salt and pepper to taste

DIRECTIONS

1. In a large pot, heat the olive oil over medium heat. Add the onion and garlic, and sauté until softened, about 5 minutes.
2. Add the cumin and turmeric, and cook for another minute.
3. Stir in the butternut squash, red lentils, and vegetable broth. Bring to a boil, then reduce the heat and simmer for 20-25 minutes, or until the squash and lentils are tender.
4. Use an immersion blender to blend the soup until smooth.
5. Season with salt and pepper to taste. Serve warm.

Ingredient Tips:

- Butternut Squash: Low glycemic index, high in fiber and vitamins.
- Red Lentils: High in protein and fiber, promoting a steady release of glucose.
- Olive Oil: Adds healthy fats that enhance satiety.

Nutrient Content (per serving):

- Calories: 300
- Total Fat: 10g
- Protein: 12g
- Carbohydrates: 40g
- Sugars: 8g
- Fiber: 10g
- Sodium: 450mg

BLACK BEAN AND QUINOA SOUP

Servings: 4 | Prep Time: 15 mins | Cook Time: 20mins | Carbs per Serving: 45g

INGREDIENTS

- 1 cup quinoa, rinsed
- 1 can black beans, rinsed and drained
- 6 cups vegetable broth
- 1 onion, chopped
- 2 garlic cloves, minced
- 1 red bell pepper, chopped
- 1 tsp cumin
- 1 tsp paprika
- 2 tbsp olive oil
- Salt and pepper to taste

DIRECTIONS

1. In a large pot, heat the olive oil over medium heat. Add the onion, garlic, and red bell pepper, and sauté until softened, about 5 minutes.
2. Add the cumin and paprika, and cook for another minute.
3. Stir in the quinoa, black beans, and vegetable broth. Bring to a boil, then reduce the heat and simmer for 20 minutes, or until the quinoa is cooked.
4. Season with salt and pepper to taste. Serve warm.

Ingredient Tips:

- Quinoa: High in protein and fiber, with a low

Nutrient Content (per serving):

- Calories: 320
- Total Fat: 10g
- Protein: 14g
- Carbohydrates: 45g
- Sugars: 5g
- Fiber: 12g
- Sodium: 400mg

TOMATO AND WHITE BEAN SOUP

Servings: 4 | Prep Time: 15 mins | Cook Time: 20 mins | Carbs per Serving: 32g

INGREDIENTS

- 1 can white beans, rinsed and drained
- 6 cups vegetable broth
- 1 onion, chopped
- 2 garlic cloves, minced
- 1 can diced tomatoes
- 2 carrots, chopped
- 2 celery stalks, chopped
- 2 tbsp olive oil
- 1 tsp thyme
- 1 tsp basil
- Salt and pepper to taste

DIRECTIONS

1. In a large pot, heat the olive oil over medium heat. Add the onion, garlic, carrots, and celery, and sauté until softened, about 5 minutes.
2. Add the thyme and basil, and cook for another minute.
3. Stir in the diced tomatoes, white beans, and vegetable broth. Bring to a boil, then reduce the heat and simmer for 20 minutes.
4. Season with salt and pepper to taste. Serve warm.

Ingredient Tips:

- White Beans: High in protein and fiber, promoting a steady release of glucose.
- Diced Tomatoes: Low glycemic index, rich in vitamins and antioxidants.
- Olive Oil: Adds healthy fats that enhance satiety.

Nutrient Content (per serving):

- Calories: 230
- Total Fat: 8g
- Protein: 10g
- Carbohydrates: 32g
- Sugars: 8g
- Fiber: 9g
- Sodium: 450mg

CHICKPEA AND SPINACH SOUP

Servings: 4 | Prep Time: 15 mins | Cook Time: 25mins | Carbs per Serving: 35g

INGREDIENTS

- 1 can chickpeas, rinsed and drained
- 6 cups vegetable broth
- 1 onion, chopped
- 2 garlic cloves, minced
- 2 cups fresh spinach, chopped
- 2 carrots, chopped
- 2 celery stalks, chopped
- 2 tbsp olive oil
- 1 tsp cumin
- 1 tsp coriander
- Salt and pepper to taste

DIRECTIONS

1. In a large pot, heat the olive oil over medium heat Add the onion, garlic, carrots, and celery, and sauté until softened, about 5 minutes.
2. Add the cumin and coriander, and cook for another minute.
3. Stir in the chickpeas and vegetable broth. Bring to a boil, then reduce the heat and simmer for 20 minutes.
4. Add the spinach and cook for another 5 minutes.
5. Season with salt and pepper to taste. Serve warm.

Ingredient Tips:

- Chickpeas: High in protein and fiber, providing a steady release of glucose

Nutrient Content (per serving):

- Calories: 280
- Total Fat: 10g
- Protein: 12g
- Carbohydrates: 35g
- Sugars: 6g
- Fiber: 10g
- Sodium: 420mg

KALE AND CANNELLINI BEAN SOUP

Servings: 4 | Prep Time: 15 mins | Cook Time: 25 mins | Carbs per Serving: 32g

INGREDIENTS

- 1 can cannellini beans, rinsed and drained
- 6 cups vegetable broth
- 1 onion, chopped
- 2 garlic cloves, minced
- 2 carrots, chopped
- 2 celery stalks, chopped
- 4 cups kale, chopped
- 2 tbsp olive oil
- 1 tsp thyme
- 1 tsp rosemary
- Salt and pepper to taste

DIRECTIONS

1. In a large pot, heat the olive oil over medium heat. Add the onion, garlic, carrots, and celery, and sauté until softened, about 5 minutes.
2. Add the thyme and rosemary, and cook for another minute.
3. Stir in the cannellini beans and vegetable broth. Bring to a boil, then reduce the heat and simmer for 20 minutes.
4. Add the kale and cook for another 5 minutes.
5. Season with salt and pepper to taste. Serve warm.

Ingredient Tips:

- Cannellini Beans: High in protein and fiber, promoting steady glucose release.
- Kale: Low glycemic index, high in vitamins and fiber.
- Olive Oil: Adds healthy fats that enhance satiety.

Nutrient Content (per serving):

- Calories: 240
- Total Fat: 9g
- Protein: 10g
- Carbohydrates: 32g
- Sugars: 5g
- Fiber: 10g
- Sodium: 450mg

BROCCOLI AND ALMOND SOUP

Servings: 4 | Prep Time: 15 mins | Cook Time: 20mins | Carbs per Serving: 20g

INGREDIENTS

- 2 cups broccoli florets
- 1/2 cup almonds, blanched
- 6 cups vegetable broth
- 1 onion, chopped
- 2 garlic cloves, minced
- 2 tbsp olive oil
- 1 tsp thyme
- Salt and pepper to taste

DIRECTIONS

1. In a large pot, heat the olive oil over medium heat. Add the onion and garlic, and sauté until softened, about 5 minutes.
2. Add the thyme and cook for another minute.
3. Stir in the broccoli and vegetable broth. Bring to a boil, then reduce the heat and simmer for 15-20 minutes, or until the broccoli is tender.
4. Add the blanched almonds and use an immersion blender to blend the soup until smooth.
5. Season with salt and pepper to taste. Serve warm.

Ingredient Tips:

- Broccoli: Low glycemic index, high in fiber and vitamins.
- Almonds: Provide healthy fats and protein, enhancing satiety and steady glucose release.
- Olive Oil: Adds healthy fats that enhance satiety.

Nutrient Content (per serving):

- Calories: 250
- Total Fat: 16g
- Protein: 8g
- Carbohydrates: 20g
- Sugars: 5g
- Fiber: 8g
- Sodium: 400mg

CARROT AND GINGER SOUP

Servings: 4 | Prep Time: 15 mins | Cook Time: 25 mins | Carbs per Serving: 30g

INGREDIENTS

- 6 large carrots, chopped
- 1 onion, chopped
- 2 garlic cloves, minced
- 1 tbsp fresh ginger, grated
- 6 cups vegetable broth
- 2 tbsp olive oil
- 1 tsp cumin
- Salt and pepper to taste

DIRECTIONS

1. In a large pot, heat the olive oil over medium heat. Add the onion, garlic, and ginger, and sauté until softened, about 5 minutes.
2. Add the cumin and cook for another minute.
3. Stir in the carrots and vegetable broth. Bring to a boil, then reduce the heat and simmer for 20-25 minutes, or until the carrots are tender.
4. Use an immersion blender to blend the soup until smooth.
5. Season with salt and pepper to taste. Serve warm.

Ingredient Tips:

- Carrots: Low glycemic index, high in vitamins and fiber.
- Ginger: Anti-inflammatory properties and adds a unique flavor.
- Olive Oil: Adds healthy fats that enhance satiety.

Nutrient Content (per serving):

- Calories: 220
- Total Fat: 10g
- Protein: 3g
- Carbohydrates: 30g
- Sugars: 14g
- Fiber: 8g
- Sodium: 400mg

MUSHROOM AND BARLEY SOUP

Servings: 4 | Prep Time: 15 mins | Cook Time: 35mins | Carbs per Serving: 50g

INGREDIENTS

- 1 cup pearl barley, rinsed
- 6 cups vegetable broth
- 1 lb mushrooms, sliced
- 1 onion, chopped
- 2 garlic cloves, minced
- 2 carrots, chopped
- 2 celery stalks, chopped
- 2 tbsp olive oil
- 1 tsp thyme
- 1 tsp rosemary
- Salt and pepper to taste

DIRECTIONS

1. In a large pot, heat the olive oil over medium heat. Add the onion, garlic, carrots, and celery, and sauté until softened, about 5 minutes.
2. Add the mushrooms, thyme, and rosemary, and cook until the mushrooms are browned, about 5 minutes.
3. Stir in the barley and vegetable broth. Bring to a boil, then reduce the heat and simmer for 30-35 minutes, or until the barley is tender.
4. Season with salt and pepper to taste. Serve warm.

Ingredient Tips:

- Barley: High in fiber, with a low glycemic index, providing steady energy release.
- Mushrooms: Low glycemic index, rich in vitamins and minerals.
- Olive Oil: Adds healthy fats that enhance satiety.

Nutrient Content (per serving):

- Calories: 320
- Total Fat: 10g
- Protein: 10g
- Carbohydrates: 50g
- Sugars: 8g
- Fiber: 10g
- Sodium: 450mg

KALE AND WHITE BEAN SOUP

Servings: 4 | Prep Time: 15 mins | Cook Time: 25 mins | Carbs per Serving: 30g

INGREDIENTS

- 1 can white beans, rinsed and drained
- 6 cups vegetable broth
- 1 onion, chopped
- 2 garlic cloves, minced
- 4 cups kale, chopped
- 2 carrots, chopped
- 2 celery stalks, chopped
- 2 tbsp olive oil
- 1 tsp thyme
- 1 tsp oregano
- Salt and pepper to taste

DIRECTIONS

1. In a large pot, heat the olive oil over medium heat. Add the onion, garlic, carrots, and celery, and sauté until softened, about 5 minutes.
2. Add the thyme and oregano, and cook for another minute.
3. Stir in the white beans and vegetable broth. Bring to a boil, then reduce the heat and simmer for 20 minutes.
4. Add the kale and cook for another 5 minutes.
5. Season with salt and pepper to taste. Serve warm.

Ingredient Tips:

- White Beans: High in protein and fiber, providing a steady release of glucose.
- Kale: Low glycemic index, high in vitamins and fiber.
- Olive Oil: Adds healthy fats that enhance satiety.

Nutrient Content (per serving):

- Calories: 240
- Total Fat: 10g
- Protein: 12g
- Carbohydrates: 30g
- Sugars: 6g
- Fiber: 10g
- Sodium: 450mg

SWEET POTATO AND BLACK BEAN SOUP

Servings: 4 | Prep Time: 15 mins | Cook Time: 30mins | Carbs per Serving: 40g

INGREDIENTS

- 2 large sweet potatoes, peeled and diced
- 1 can black beans, rinsed and drained
- 6 cups vegetable broth
- 1 onion, chopped
- 2 garlic cloves, minced
- 1 tsp cumin
- 1 tsp smoked paprika
- 2 tbsp olive oil
- Salt and pepper to taste

DIRECTIONS

1. In a large pot, heat the olive oil over medium heat Add the onion and garlic, and sauté until softened about 5 minutes.
2. Add the cumin and smoked paprika, and cook for another minute.
3. Stir in the sweet potatoes, black beans, and vegetable broth. Bring to a boil, then reduce the heat and simmer for 25-30 minutes, or until the sweet potatoes are tender.
4. Season with salt and pepper to taste. Serve warm.

Ingredient Tips:

- Sweet Potatoes: High in fiber and vitamins, with a low glycemic index.
- Black Beans: High in protein and fiber, providing a steady release of glucose.
- Olive Oil: Adds healthy fats that enhance satiety.

Nutrient Content (per serving):

- Calories: 280
- Total Fat: 8g
- Protein: 8g
- Carbohydrates: 40g
- Sugars: 8g
- Fiber: 8g
- Sodium: 420mg

ZUCCHINI AND CHICKPEA SOUP

Servings: 4 | Prep Time: 15 mins | Cook Time: 20 mins | Carbs per Serving: 28g

INGREDIENTS

- 1 can chickpeas, rinsed and drained
- 6 cups vegetable broth
- 1 onion, chopped
- 2 garlic cloves, minced
- 2 large zucchinis, chopped
- 2 carrots, chopped
- 2 celery stalks, chopped
- 2 tbsp olive oil
- 1 tsp thyme
- 1 tsp oregano
- Salt and pepper to taste

DIRECTIONS

1. In a large pot, heat the olive oil over medium heat. Add the onion, garlic, carrots, and celery, and sauté until softened, about 5 minutes.
2. Add the thyme and oregano, and cook for another minute.
3. Stir in the chickpeas, zucchinis, and vegetable broth. Bring to a boil, then reduce the heat and simmer for 20 minutes.
4. Season with salt and pepper to taste. Serve warm.

Ingredient Tips:

- Chickpeas: High in protein and fiber, providing a steady release of glucose.
- Zucchini: Low glycemic index, high in vitamins and fiber.
- Olive Oil: Adds healthy fats that enhance satiety.

Nutrient Content (per serving):

- Calories: 240
- Total Fat: 10g
- Protein: 10g
- Carbohydrates: 28g
- Sugars: 7g
- Fiber: 8g
- Sodium: 430mg

Chapter Seven

Diabetic Friendly Snacks Recipes

ALMOND BUTTER AND CELERY STICKS

Servings: 2 | Prep Time: 5 mins | Cook Time: 0mins | Carbs per Serving: 8g

INGREDIENTS

- 4 celery stalks, cut into sticks
- 1/4 cup almond butter (unsweetened)

DIRECTIONS

1. Wash the celery stalks and cut them into sticks.
2. Spread a tablespoon of almond butter on each celery stick.
3. Serve immediately.

Ingredient Tips:

- Almond Butter: Provides protein and healthy fats, promoting satiety and steady glucose levels.
- Celery: Low glycemic index, high in fiber and water content.

Nutrient Content (per serving):

- Calories: 150
- Total Fat: 12g
- Protein: 4g
- Carbohydrates: 8g
- Sugars: 2g
- Fiber: 4g
- Sodium: 70mg

GREEK YOGURT WITH CHIA SEEDS AND BERRIES

Servings: 1 | Prep Time: 5 mins | Cook Time: 0 mins | Carbs per Serving: 20g

INGREDIENTS

- 1 cup Greek yogurt (5% fat)
- 1 tbsp chia seeds
- 1/2 cup mixed berries (blueberries, raspberries)

DIRECTIONS

1. In a bowl, mix the Greek yogurt with chia seeds.
2. Top with fresh berries.
3. Serve immediately.

Ingredient Tips:

- Greek Yogurt: High in protein and healthy fats, which help stabilize glucose levels.
- Chia Seeds: High in fiber, aiding in steady glucose release.
- Berries: Low glycemic index, rich in antioxidants and vitamins.

Nutrient Content (per serving):

- Calories: 250
- Total Fat: 12g
- Protein: 15g
- Carbohydrates: 20g
- Sugars: 12g
- Fiber: 8g
- Sodium: 80mg

AVOCADO AND BLACK BEAN SALSA

Servings: 2 | Prep Time: 10 mins | Cook Time: 0mins | Carbs per Serving: 18g

INGREDIENTS

- 1 avocado, diced
- 1/2 cup black beans, cooked
- 1/4 cup red onion, finely chopped
- 1/4 cup cilantro, chopped
- 1 tbsp lime juice
- Salt and pepper to taste

DIRECTIONS

1. In a bowl, combine the diced avocado, black beans, red onion, and cilantro.
2. Drizzle with lime juice and season with salt and pepper.
3. Serve immediately.

Ingredient Tips:

- Avocado: Provides healthy fats and fiber, enhancing satiety and steady glucose levels.
- Black Beans: High in protein and fiber, promoting steady glucose release.
- Lime Juice: Adds a refreshing flavor and aids in the absorption of nutrients.

Nutrient Content (per serving):

- Calories: 180
- Total Fat: 10g
- Protein: 5g
- Carbohydrates: 18g
- Sugars: 1g
- Fiber: 8g
- Sodium: 180mg

SPICED ROASTED CHICKPEAS

Servings: 4 | Prep Time: 5 mins | Cook Time: 25 mins | Carbs per Serving: 18g

INGREDIENTS

- 1 can chickpeas, rinsed and drained
- 2 tbsp olive oil
- 1 tsp paprika
- 1/2 tsp cumin
- 1/2 tsp garlic powder
- Salt and pepper to taste

DIRECTIONS

1. Preheat the oven to 400°F (200°C).
2. In a bowl, toss the chickpeas with olive oil and spices.
3. Spread the chickpeas on a baking sheet in a single layer.
4. Roast for 20-25 minutes, or until crispy, shaking the pan halfway through.
5. Let cool slightly and serve.

Ingredient Tips:

- Chickpeas: High in protein and fiber, providing a steady release of glucose.
- Olive Oil: Adds healthy fats that enhance satiety.
- Spices: Enhance flavor without adding calories or sugar.

Nutrient Content (per serving):

- Calories: 160
- Total Fat: 7g
- Protein: 5g
- Carbohydrates: 18g
- Sugars: 1g
- Fiber: 6g
- Sodium: 200mg

SPICED CHICKPEA AND AVOCADO TOAST

Servings: 4 | Prep Time: 10 mins | Cook Time: 10mins | Carbs per Serving: 28g

INGREDIENTS

- 1 can chickpeas, rinsed and drained
- 1 avocado
- 1 tsp cumin
- 1 tsp paprika
- 1 tsp olive oil
- 1 tsp lemon juice
- Salt and pepper to taste
- 4 slices of rye or spelt bread

DIRECTIONS

1. In a bowl, mash the avocado with lemon juice, salt, and pepper.
2. In a pan, heat the olive oil over medium heat. Add the chickpeas, cumin, and paprika. Cook for 5-7 minutes until the chickpeas are slightly crispy.
3. Toast the slices of bread.
4. Spread the mashed avocado on each slice of toast, then top with spiced chickpeas.
5. Serve immediately.

Ingredient Tips:

- Chickpeas: High in protein and fiber, providing a steady release of glucose.
- Avocado: Rich in healthy fats and fiber, promoting satiety and steady energy.
- Rye or Spelt Bread: Lower glycemic index compared to wheat-based bread.

Nutrient Content (per serving):

- Calories: 290
- Total Fat: 14g
- Protein: 8g
- Carbohydrates: 28g
- Sugars: 2g
- Fiber: 10g
- Sodium: 320mg

GREEK YOGURT WITH NUTS AND SEEDS

Servings: 1 | Prep Time: 5 mins | Cook Time: 0 mins | Carbs per Serving: 12g

INGREDIENTS

- 1 cup Greek yogurt (5% fat)
- 1 tbsp chia seeds
- 1 tbsp flaxseeds
- 1 tbsp almonds, chopped
- 1 tbsp walnuts, chopped

DIRECTIONS

1. In a bowl, mix the Greek yogurt with chia seeds and flaxseeds.
2. Top with chopped almonds and walnuts.
3. Serve immediately.

Ingredient Tips:

- Greek Yogurt: High in protein and healthy fats, helping to stabilize blood sugar levels.
- Chia and Flaxseeds: Rich in fiber and omega-3 fatty acids, promoting satiety and heart health.
- Nuts: Provide healthy fats and protein, enhancing satiety.

Nutrient Content (per serving):

- Calories: 320
- Total Fat: 20g
- Protein: 18g
- Carbohydrates: 12g
- Sugars: 6g
- Fiber: 6g
- Sodium: 100mg

SPICED ROASTED NUTS

Servings: 8 | Prep Time: 5 mins | Cook Time: 12 mins | Carbs per Serving: 6g

INGREDIENTS

- 1 cup almonds
- 1 cup walnuts
- 1 tsp cumin
- 1 tsp paprika
- 1/2 tsp garlic powder
- 1/2 tsp salt
- 1 tbsp olive oil

DIRECTIONS

1. Preheat the oven to 350°F (175°C).
2. In a bowl, mix the almonds and walnuts with olive oil, cumin, paprika, garlic powder, and salt.
3. Spread the nuts on a baking sheet and roast for 10-12 minutes, stirring occasionally.
4. Let cool before serving.

Ingredient Tips:

- Nuts: High in healthy fats and protein, promoting satiety and steady glucose release.
- Spices: Add flavor without adding sugars or high glycemic ingredients.

Nutrient Content (per serving):

- Calories: 200
- Total Fat: 18g
- Protein: 5g
- Carbohydrates: 6g
- Sugars: 1g
- Fiber: 4g
- Sodium: 100mg

EDAMAME HUMMUS WITH VEGGIE STICKS

Servings: 4 | Prep Time: 10 mins | Cook Time: 0 mins | Carbs per Serving: 16g

INGREDIENTS

- 2 cups shelled edamame
- 2 tbsp tahini
- 2 tbsp lemon juice
- 2 garlic cloves, minced
- 2 tbsp olive oil
- 1/2 tsp salt
- 1/4 tsp pepper
- Assorted veggie sticks (carrots, cucumbers, bell peppers)

DIRECTIONS

1. In a food processor, blend the edamame, tahini, lemon juice, garlic, olive oil, salt, and pepper until smooth.
2. Serve the hummus with assorted veggie sticks.

Ingredient Tips:

- Edamame: High in protein and fiber, promoting a steady release of glucose.
- Tahini: Adds healthy fats and enhances the flavor of the hummus.
- Veggie Sticks: Low glycemic index and high in fiber, vitamins, and minerals.

Nutrient Content (per serving):

- Calories: 220
- Total Fat: 12g
- Protein: 10g
- Carbohydrates: 16g
- Sugars: 3g
- Fiber: 6g
- Sodium: 300mg

Chapter Eight

Diabetic Friendly Desserts Recipes

CHIA SEED PUDDING WITH BERRIES

Servings: 2 | Prep Time: 15 mins | Cook Time: 0 mins | Carbs per Serving: 15g

INGREDIENTS

- 1/4 cup chia seeds
- 1 cup unsweetened almond milk
- 1/2 teaspoon vanilla extract
- 1 tablespoon almond butter
- 1 cup mixed berries (e.g., strawberries, blueberries)
- 1 tablespoon chopped nuts (optional)

DIRECTIONS

1. In a bowl, combine chia seeds, almond milk, and vanilla extract. Stir well and let sit for 10 minutes, stirring occasionally until thickened.
2. Layer chia seed mixture with almond butter and berries in serving glasses.
3. Top with chopped nuts if desired. Serve chilled.

Ingredient Tips:

This chia seed pudding is a delightful, fiber-rich dessert featuring healthy fats from almond butter and antioxidants from mixed berries, perfect for satisfying cravings without spiking blood sugar.

Nutrient Content (per serving):

- Calories: 250
- Total Fat: 15g
- Protein: 7g
- Carbohydrates: 25g
- Sugars: 5g
- Fiber: 10g
- Sodium: 80mg

AVOCADO CHOCOLATE MOUSSE

Servings: 4 | Prep Time: 10 mins | Cook Time: 0 mins | Carbs per Serving: 15g

INGREDIENTS

- 2 ripe avocados
- 1/4 cup unsweetened cocoa powder
- 1/4 cup coconut milk
- 2 tablespoons honey (optional, adjust to taste)
- 1 teaspoon vanilla extract

DIRECTIONS

1. Blend avocados, cocoa powder, coconut milk, honey (if using), and vanilla extract until smooth and creamy.
2. Chill in the refrigerator for 30 minutes before serving.
3. Garnish with fresh berries or chopped nuts if desired.

Ingredient Tips:

- This creamy avocado chocolate mousse is rich in healthy fats and antioxidants from cocoa, providing a decadent yet diabetes-friendly dessert option.

Nutrient Content (per serving):

- Calories: 200
- Total Fat: 15g
- Protein: 3g
- Carbohydrates: 20g
- Sugars: 8g
- Fiber: 7g
- Sodium: 10mg

COCONUT YOGURT PARFAIT

Servings: 2 | Prep Time: 10 mins | Cook Time: 0 mins | Carbs per Serving: 20g

INGREDIENTS

- 1 cup unsweetened coconut yogurt
- 1/2 cup mixed berries
- 2 tablespoons chopped nuts (e.g., almonds, walnuts)
- 1 tablespoon chia seeds
- 1 teaspoon honey (optional, adjust to taste)

DIRECTIONS

1. Layer coconut yogurt, mixed berries, chopped nuts, and chia seeds in serving glasses or bowls.
2. Drizzle with honey if desired. Serve chilled.

Ingredient Tips:

This coconut yogurt parfait combines creamy yogurt with fiber-rich berries and nuts, offering a satisfying and nutritious dessert option for managing blood sugar levels.

Nutrient Content (per serving):

- Calories: 180
- Total Fat: 10g
- Protein: 5g
- Carbohydrates: 20g
- Sugars: 10g
- Fiber: 8g
- Sodium: 20mg

BAKED APPLE WITH CINNAMON AND ALMONDS

Servings: 2 | Prep Time: 10 mins | Cook Time: 30 mins | Carbs per Serving: 25g

INGREDIENTS

- 2 apples (preferably Granny Smith or Fuji)
- 1 tablespoon chopped almonds
- 1 teaspoon ground cinnamon
- 1 tablespoon honey (optional, adjust to taste)

DIRECTIONS

1. Preheat the oven to 375°F (190°C).
2. Core the apples and place them on a baking dish.
3. Mix chopped almonds with cinnamon and stuff the mixture into the apples' cores.
4. Drizzle honey over the apples if desired.
5. Bake for 25-30 minutes or until the apples are tender.
6. Serve warm, optionally with a dollop of Greek yogurt or coconut cream.

Ingredient Tips:

- This baked apple dessert is naturally sweetened with a hint of honey, topped with crunchy almonds and cinnamon, providing a comforting treat that's gentle on blood sugar levels.

Nutrient Content (per serving):

- Calories: 180
- Total Fat: 5g
- Protein: 2g
- Carbohydrates: 35g
- Sugars: 25g
- Fiber: 5g
- Sodium: 0mg

LEMON BLUEBERRY YOGURT BARK

Servings: 4 | Prep Time: 10 mins | Cook Time: 0 mins | Carbs per Serving: 10g

INGREDIENTS

- 1 cup plain Greek yogurt (5% fat)
- Zest of 1 lemon
- 1 tablespoon lemon juice
- 1 tablespoon honey (optional, adjust to taste)
- 1/2 cup fresh blueberries

DIRECTIONS

1. Line a baking sheet with parchment paper.
2. In a bowl, mix Greek yogurt, lemon zest, lemon juice, and honey until smooth.
3. Spread the yogurt mixture evenly onto the prepared baking sheet.
4. Sprinkle fresh blueberries over the yogurt.
5. Freeze for 2-3 hours until firm.
6. Break into pieces before serving.

Ingredient Tips:

This refreshing yogurt bark combines tangy lemon with sweet blueberries, offering a guilt-free dessert option packed with protein and antioxidants.

Nutrient Content (per serving):

- Calories: 120
- Total Fat: 4g
- Protein: 8g
- Carbohydrates: 15g
- Sugars: 12g
- Fiber: 1g
- Sodium: 30mg

ALMOND FLOUR CHOCOLATE CHIP COOKIES

Servings: 12 | Prep Time: 15 mins | Cook Time: 10 mins | Carbs per Serving: 15g

INGREDIENTS

- 1 1/2 cups almond flour
- 1/4 teaspoon baking soda
- 1/4 teaspoon salt
- 1/4 cup coconut oil, melted
- 1/4 cup honey (or maple syrup)
- 1 teaspoon vanilla extract
- 1/4 cup dark chocolate chips (at least 70% cocoa)

DIRECTIONS

1. Preheat the oven to 350°F (175°C). Line a baking sheet with parchment paper.
2. In a bowl, whisk together almond flour, baking soda, and salt.
3. In a separate bowl, mix melted coconut oil, honey, and vanilla extract.
4. Combine wet and dry ingredients until well incorporated.
5. Fold in dark chocolate chips.
6. Scoop dough into tablespoon-sized balls and place them on the baking sheet.
7. Flatten each ball slightly with a fork.
8. Bake for 10-12 minutes until golden brown.
9. Allow cookies to cool on the baking sheet for 5 minutes before transferring to a wire rack to cool completely.

Ingredient Tips:

- These almond flour chocolate chip cookies are a healthier twist on a classic favorite, using almond flour and honey for sweetness, making them suitable for managing blood sugar levels.

Nutrient Content (per serving):

- Calories: 150
- Total Fat: 10g
- Protein: 3g
- Carbohydrates: 15g
- Sugars: 10g
- Fiber: 2g
- Sodium: 60mg

CHIA SEED PUDDING WITH BERRIES

Servings: 2 | Prep Time: 5 mins | Cook Time: 0 mins | Carbs per Serving: 20g

INGREDIENTS

- 1/4 cup chia seeds
- 1 cup unsweetened almond milk
- 1/2 teaspoon vanilla extract
- 1 tablespoon honey (optional, adjust to taste)
- 1/2 cup mixed berries (such as strawberries, blueberries, raspberries)

DIRECTIONS

1. In a bowl, mix chia seeds, almond milk, vanilla extract, and honey (if using). Stir well to combine.
2. Let the mixture sit for 10 minutes, then stir again to break up any clumps of chia seeds.
3. Cover and refrigerate for at least 2 hours or overnight, until the mixture thickens into a pudding-like consistency.
4. Stir the pudding before serving and top with mixed berries.

Ingredient Tips:

This chia seed pudding offers a creamy texture with a burst of fresh berries, providing a satisfying dessert option rich in fiber and antioxidants.

Nutrient Content (per serving):

- Calories: 180
- Total Fat: 9g
- Protein: 5g
- Carbohydrates: 25g
- Sugars: 10g
- Fiber: 10g
- Sodium: 80mg

AVOCADO CHOCOLATE MOUSSE

Servings: 4 | Prep Time: 10 mins | Cook Time: 0 mins | Carbs per Serving: 20g

INGREDIENTS

- 2 ripe avocados
- 1/4 cup unsweetened cocoa powder
- 1/4 cup honey or maple syrup
- 1 teaspoon vanilla extract
- Pinch of salt
- Fresh berries for garnish (optional)

DIRECTIONS

1. Scoop the flesh of the avocados into a blender or food processor.
2. Add cocoa powder, honey or maple syrup, vanilla extract, and a pinch of salt.
3. Blend until smooth and creamy, scraping down the sides as needed.
4. Taste and adjust sweetness if necessary.
5. Transfer the mousse to serving bowls and chill in the refrigerator for at least 30 minutes.
6. Serve chilled, garnished with fresh berries if desired.

Ingredient Tips:

- This creamy avocado chocolate mousse is a decadent yet healthy dessert option, rich in heart-healthy fats and antioxidants from cocoa and avocado.

Nutrient Content (per serving):

- Calories: 220
- Total Fat: 14g
- Protein: 3g
- Carbohydrates: 25g
- Sugars: 15g
- Fiber: 7g
- Sodium: 10mg

COCONUT FLOUR LEMON BARS

Servings: 12 | Prep Time: 15 mins | Cook Time: 35 mins | Carbs per Serving: 15g

INGREDIENTS

For the crust:
- 1 cup coconut flour
- 1/4 cup coconut oil, melted
- 2 tablespoons honey or maple syrup
- Pinch of salt

For the filling:
- 4 eggs
- Zest and juice of 2 lemons
- 1/4 cup honey or maple syrup
- 1/4 cup coconut flour
- 1/2 teaspoon baking powder

Nutrient Content (per serving):
- Calories: 180
- Total Fat: 10g
- Protein: 4g
- Carbohydrates: 20g
- Sugars: 10g
- Fiber: 5g
- Sodium: 50mg

DIRECTIONS

1. Preheat the oven to 350°F (175°C). Grease or line an 8x8 inch baking pan with parchment paper.
2. In a bowl, combine coconut flour, melted coconut oil, honey or maple syrup, and a pinch of salt to make the crust. Mix until crumbly.
3. Press the crust mixture evenly into the bottom of the prepared baking pan.
4. Bake the crust for 10 minutes until lightly golden. Remove from the oven and let it cool slightly.
5. Meanwhile, prepare the filling. In a bowl, whisk together eggs, lemon zest, lemon juice, honey or maple syrup, coconut flour, and baking powder until smooth.
6. Pour the filling over the baked crust and spread evenly.
7. Bake for 20-25 minutes or until the filling is set and the edges are lightly golden.
8. Allow the bars to cool completely in the pan before slicing into squares.
9. Refrigerate leftovers in an airtight container.

Ingredient Tips:

These coconut flour lemon bars are a delightful treat with a tangy lemon filling and a coconut flour crust, providing a lower-carb option with a burst of citrus flavor.

CINNAMON WALNUT BAKED APPLES

Servings: 4 | Prep Time: 10 mins | Cook Time: 0 mins | Carbs per Serving: 20g

INGREDIENTS

- 4 medium-sized apples (such as Granny Smith or Honeycrisp)
- 1/2 cup chopped walnuts
- 2 tablespoons melted coconut oil or butter
- 2 tablespoons honey or maple syrup
- 1 teaspoon ground cinnamon
- 1/4 teaspoon nutmeg
- Pinch of salt
- Greek yogurt or whipped coconut cream for serving (optional)

DIRECTIONS

1. Preheat the oven to 375°F (190°C). Core each apple and scoop out a bit of the center to create a well for filling.
2. In a bowl, mix chopped walnuts, melted coconut oil or butter, honey or maple syrup, cinnamon, nutmeg, and a pinch of salt until well combined.
3. Stuff each apple with the walnut mixture, pressing gently to pack it in.
4. Place the stuffed apples in a baking dish. Pour about 1/4 cup of water into the bottom of the dish to create steam while baking.
5. Bake for 30-40 minutes, or until the apples are tender and the filling is golden and bubbly.
6. Remove from the oven and let cool slightly before serving.
7. Serve warm, optionally topped with a dollop of Greek yogurt or whipped coconut cream.

Nutrient Content (per serving):
- Calories: 220
- Total Fat: 12g
- Protein: 3g
- Carbohydrates: 35g
- Sugars: 25g
- Fiber: 5g
- Sodium: 10mg

Ingredient Tips:

These cinnamon walnut baked apples are a comforting dessert with warm spices and crunchy nuts, perfect for a cozy evening treat without spiking blood sugar levels.

BERRY YOGURT PARFAIT

Servings: 2 | Prep Time: 5 mins | Cook Time: 0 mins | Carbs per Serving: 20g

INGREDIENTS

- 1 cup Greek yogurt (unsweetened)
- 1 cup mixed berries (such as strawberries, blueberries, raspberries)
- 1/4 cup chopped nuts (such as almonds, walnuts)
- 1 tablespoon chia seeds (optional)
- 1 tablespoon honey or maple syrup (optional, adjust to taste)

DIRECTIONS

1. In a serving glass or bowl, layer Greek yogurt, mixed berries, chopped nuts, and chia seeds (if using).
2. Drizzle with honey or maple syrup if desired for added sweetness.
3. Repeat the layers until the glass or bowl is filled.
4. Serve immediately or refrigerate until ready to eat.

Nutrient Content (per serving):
- Calories: 200
- Total Fat: 10g
- Protein: 15g
- Carbohydrates: 25g
- Sugars: 15g
- Fiber: 5g
- Sodium: 50mg

Ingredient Tips:
This berry yogurt parfait is a refreshing and nutritious dessert or snack option, combining creamy Greek yogurt with antioxidant-rich berries and crunchy nuts.

ALMOND FLOUR PUMPKIN MUFFINS

Servings: 12 | Prep Time: 15 mins | Cook Time: 20 mins | Carbs per Serving: 15g

INGREDIENTS

- 2 cups almond flour
- 1/2 teaspoon baking soda
- 1/4 teaspoon salt
- 1 teaspoon ground cinnamon
- 1/2 teaspoon ground nutmeg
- 1/4 teaspoon ground cloves
- 1/2 cup pumpkin puree
- 1/4 cup honey or maple syrup
- 2 large eggs
- 1/4 cup melted coconut oil or butter
- 1 teaspoon vanilla extract
- 1/2 cup chopped pecans or walnuts (optional)

DIRECTIONS

1. Preheat the oven to 350°F (175°C). Line a muffin tin with paper liners or grease well.
2. In a bowl, whisk together almond flour, baking soda, salt, cinnamon, nutmeg, and cloves.
3. In another bowl, mix pumpkin puree, honey or maple syrup, eggs, melted coconut oil or butter, and vanilla extract until smooth.
4. Pour the wet ingredients into the dry ingredients and stir until just combined. Fold in chopped nuts if using.
5. Spoon the batter evenly into the prepared muffin tin, filling each cup about 3/4 full.
6. Bake for 20-25 minutes, or until a toothpick inserted into the center comes out clean.
7. Remove from the oven and let cool in the pan for 5 minutes, then transfer muffins to a wire rack to cool completely.

Nutrient Content (per serving):
- Calories: 220
- Total Fat: 15g
- Protein: 6g
- Carbohydrates: 20g
- Sugars: 10g
- Fiber: 5g
- Sodium: 150mg

Ingredient Tips:
These almond flour pumpkin muffins are moist and flavorful, perfect for a healthier option that satisfies cravings without causing blood sugar spikes.

Chapter Nine

Diabetic Friendly Dinner Recipes

GRILLED LEMON HERB CHICKEN WITH QUINOA

Servings: 4 | Prep Time: 30 mins | Cook Time: 25 mins | Carbs per Serving: 28g

INGREDIENTS

- 4 boneless, skinless chicken breasts
- 1/4 cup olive oil
- Juice of 2 lemons
- 3 garlic cloves, minced
- 2 tablespoons fresh parsley, chopped
- 1 tablespoon fresh thyme, chopped
- Salt and pepper to taste
- 1 cup quinoa
- 2 cups water or low-sodium chicken broth
- 4 cups broccoli florets
- Lemon wedges for serving

DIRECTIONS

1. In a bowl, mix olive oil, lemon juice, garlic, parsley, thyme, salt, and pepper. Add chicken breasts and marinate for at least 30 minutes.
2. Cook quinoa: Rinse quinoa under cold water. In a medium pot, bring water or broth to a boil, add quinoa, reduce heat, cover, and simmer for 15 minutes until liquid is absorbed.
3. Steam broccoli: Place broccoli in a steamer basket over boiling water, cover, and steam for about 5 minutes until tender.
4. Preheat grill to medium-high heat. Grill chicken for 6-7 minutes on each side until fully cooked.
5. Serve chicken with quinoa and broccoli, garnished with lemon wedges.

Nutrient Content (per serving):

- Calories: 450
- Total Fat: 20g
- Protein: 40g
- Carbohydrates: 28g
- Sugars: 2g
- Fiber: 5g
- Sodium: 220mg

Ingredient Tips:
A light and flavorful dinner with grilled lemon herb chicken served alongside protein-packed quinoa and nutrient-dense steamed broccoli.

SPAGHETTI SQUASH WITH TURKEY BOLOGNESE

Servings: 4 | Prep Time: 15 mins | Cook Time: 40 mins | Carbs per Serving: 15g

INGREDIENTS

- 1 large spaghetti squash
- 1 tablespoon olive oil
- 1 pound ground turkey
- 1 small onion, diced
- 3 garlic cloves, minced
- 1 can (14.5 oz) crushed tomatoes (no added sugar)
- 2 tablespoons tomato paste
- 1 teaspoon dried oregano
- 1 teaspoon dried basil
- Salt and pepper to taste
- Fresh parsley, chopped (for garnish)

DIRECTIONS

1. Preheat the oven to 400°F (200°C). Cut spaghetti squash in half lengthwise, remove seeds, drizzle with olive oil, and season with salt and pepper. Place cut side down on a baking sheet and roast for 40 minutes.
2. While the squash is roasting, heat a large skillet over medium heat. Add ground turkey, onion, and garlic. Cook until turkey is browned and onions are soft.
3. Add crushed tomatoes, tomato paste, oregano, basil, salt, and pepper. Simmer for 20 minutes.
4. Once the squash is cooked, use a fork to scrape out the flesh into spaghetti-like strands.
5. Serve the turkey bolognese sauce over the spaghetti squash and garnish with fresh parsley.

Nutrient Content (per serving):

- Calories: 320
- Total Fat: 15g
- Protein: 28g
- Carbohydrates: 15g
- Sugars: 7g
- Fiber: 5g
- Sodium: 450mg

Ingredient Tips:
A low-carb alternative to traditional spaghetti, this dish features spaghetti squash topped with a hearty turkey bolognese sauce.

LENTIL AND VEGETABLE STEW

Servings: 4 | Prep Time: 10 mins | Cook Time: 40 mins | Carbs per Serving: 35g

INGREDIENTS

- 1 cup green or brown lentils, rinsed
- 1 tablespoon olive oil
- 1 onion, diced
- 2 carrots, sliced
- 2 celery stalks, sliced
- 3 garlic cloves, minced
- 1 can (14.5 oz) diced tomatoes (no added sugar)
- 4 cups low-sodium vegetable broth
- 2 cups chopped kale or spinach
- 1 teaspoon dried thyme
- 1 teaspoon dried rosemary
- Salt and pepper to taste

DIRECTIONS

1. Heat olive oil in a large pot over medium heat. Add onion, carrots, and celery, and sauté until softened.
2. Add garlic and cook for another minute.
3. Stir in lentils, diced tomatoes, vegetable broth, thyme, rosemary, salt, and pepper. Bring to a boil, then reduce heat and simmer for 30-35 minutes until lentils are tender.
4. Add kale or spinach and cook for an additional 5 minutes until greens are wilted.
5. Serve hot.

Nutrient Content (per serving):

- Calories: 250
- Total Fat: 6g
- Protein: 12g
- Carbohydrates: 35g
- Sugars: 7g
- Fiber: 12g
- Sodium: 400mg

Ingredient Tips:

This hearty lentil and vegetable stew is packed with fiber and plant-based protein, making it a satisfying and nutritious dinner option.

BAKED SALMON WITH ASPARAGUS AND QUINOA

Servings: 4 | Prep Time: 10 mins | Cook Time: 20 mins | Carbs per Serving: 22g

INGREDIENTS

- 4 salmon fillets
- 1 tablespoon olive oil
- 2 lemons (1 for juice, 1 for slices)
- 2 garlic cloves, minced
- Salt and pepper to taste
- 1 bunch asparagus, trimmed
- 1 cup quinoa
- 2 cups water or low-sodium chicken broth

Nutrient Content (per serving):

- Calories: 450
- Total Fat: 20g
- Protein: 35g
- Carbohydrates: 22g
- Sugars: 2g
- Fiber: 5g
- Sodium: 150mg

DIRECTIONS

1. Preheat oven to 400°F (200°C). Place salmon fillets on a baking sheet lined with parchment paper. Drizzle with olive oil, lemon juice, and minced garlic. Season with salt and pepper. Arrange lemon slices on top.
2. Place asparagus around the salmon on the baking sheet. Drizzle with a little olive oil, salt, and pepper.
3. Bake for 15-20 minutes until salmon is cooked through and asparagus is tender.
4. Cook quinoa: Rinse quinoa under cold water. In a medium pot, bring water or broth to a boil, add quinoa, reduce heat, cover, and simmer for 15 minutes until liquid is absorbed.
5. Serve salmon with asparagus and quinoa.

Ingredient Tips:

A balanced dinner of baked salmon, asparagus, and quinoa that provides healthy fats, protein, and fiber, ideal for managing blood sugar levels.

STUFFED BELL PEPPERS WITH GROUND BEEF

Servings: 4 | Prep Time: 15 mins | Cook Time: 40 mins | Carbs per Serving: 30g

INGREDIENTS

- 4 large bell peppers
- 1 tablespoon olive oil
- 1 pound ground beef
- 1 small onion, diced
- 2 garlic cloves, minced
- 1 can (14.5 oz) diced tomatoes (no added sugar)
- 1 cup cooked brown rice
- 1 teaspoon dried oregano
- 1 teaspoon dried basil
- Salt and pepper to taste
- 1/2 cup shredded mozzarella cheese (optional)

DIRECTIONS

1. Preheat oven to 375°F (190°C). Cut tops off bell peppers and remove seeds.
2. Heat olive oil in a skillet over medium heat. Add ground beef, onion, and garlic. Cook until beef is browned and onions are soft.
3. Stir in diced tomatoes, cooked brown rice, oregano, basil, salt, and pepper. Cook for 5 minutes.
4. Stuff each bell pepper with the beef mixture and place in a baking dish. Top with shredded mozzarella cheese if using.
5. Cover with foil and bake for 30 minutes. Remove foil and bake for an additional 10 minutes until peppers are tender.
6. Serve hot.

Nutrient Content (per serving):

- Calories: 350
- Total Fat: 15g
- Protein: 25g
- Carbohydrates: 30g
- Sugars: 7g
- Fiber: 7g
- Sodium: 400mg

Ingredient Tips:
These stuffed bell peppers are filled with a flavorful mixture of ground beef and brown rice, making them a delicious and nutritious dinner option.

CHICKPEA AND SPINACH CURRY

Servings: 4 | Prep Time: 10 mins | Cook Time: 20 mins | Carbs per Serving: 40g

INGREDIENTS

- 1 tablespoon coconut oil
- 1 onion, diced
- 3 garlic cloves, minced
- 1 tablespoon fresh ginger, grated
- 1 tablespoon curry powder
- 1 teaspoon ground cumin
- 1 teaspoon ground coriander
- 1/2 teaspoon turmeric
- 1 can (14.5 oz) diced tomatoes (no added sugar)
- 1 can (14.5 oz) coconut milk
- 1 can (14.5 oz) chickpeas, drained and rinsed
- 4 cups fresh spinach
- Salt and pepper to taste
- Fresh cilantro, chopped (for garnish)
- Cooked brown rice or quinoa for serving

DIRECTIONS

1. Heat coconut oil in a large pot over medium heat. Add onion, garlic, and ginger. Sauté until onion is soft.
2. Stir in curry powder, cumin, coriander, and turmeric. Cook for 1 minute until fragrant.
3. Add diced tomatoes and coconut milk. Bring to a simmer.
4. Stir in chickpeas and spinach. Cook until spinach is wilted and chickpeas are heated through, about 5 minutes.
5. Season with salt and pepper to taste. Garnish with fresh cilantro.
6. Serve with cooked brown rice or quinoa.

Nutrient Content (per serving):

- Calories: 300
- Total Fat: 15g
- Protein: 10g
- Carbohydrates: 40g
- Sugars: 8g
- Fiber: 10g
- Sodium: 350mg

Ingredient Tips:
This chickpea and spinach curry is a flavorful, plant-based dinner option that is rich in fiber and healthy fats, perfect for keeping blood sugar levels stable.

BAKED COD WITH TOMATO AND OLIVE RELISH

Servings: 4 | Prep Time: 10 mins | Cook Time: 15 mins | Carbs per Serving: 8g

INGREDIENTS

- 4 cod fillets
- 1 tablespoon olive oil
- Salt and pepper to taste
- 2 cups cherry tomatoes, halved
- 1/2 cup Kalamata olives, pitted and sliced
- 1/4 cup red onion, finely chopped
- 2 garlic cloves, minced
- 2 tablespoons fresh parsley, chopped
- 1 tablespoon capers, rinsed and drained
- 1 tablespoon lemon juice

DIRECTIONS

1. Preheat oven to 400°F (200°C). Place cod fillets on a baking sheet lined with parchment paper. Drizzle with olive oil and season with salt and pepper.
2. Bake for 12-15 minutes until cod is opaque and flakes easily with a fork.
3. While the cod is baking, prepare the tomato and olive relish. In a bowl, combine cherry tomatoes, Kalamata olives, red onion, garlic, parsley, capers, and lemon juice. Mix well.
4. Serve the baked cod topped with the tomato and olive relish.

Nutrient Content (per serving):

- Calories: 200
- Total Fat: 8g
- Protein: 25g
- Carbohydrates: 8g
- Sugars: 4g
- Fiber: 2g
- Sodium: 400mg

Ingredient Tips:
Baked cod with a fresh tomato and olive relish is a light and delicious dinner option that provides lean protein and healthy fats.

QUINOA-STUFFED PORTOBELLO MUSHROOMS

Servings: 4 | Prep Time: 15 mins | Cook Time: 20 mins | Carbs per Serving: 20g

INGREDIENTS

- 4 large portobello mushrooms, stems removed
- 1 tablespoon olive oil
- 1 cup cooked quinoa
- 1 small zucchini, diced
- 1 red bell pepper, diced
- 1 small onion, diced
- 2 garlic cloves, minced
- 1/4 cup grated Parmesan cheese
- Salt and pepper to taste
- Fresh basil, chopped (for garnish)

DIRECTIONS

1. Preheat oven to 375°F (190°C). Place portobello mushrooms on a baking sheet lined with parchment paper. Drizzle with olive oil and season with salt and pepper.
2. In a skillet over medium heat, sauté zucchini, bell pepper, onion, and garlic until soft.
3. In a bowl, combine cooked quinoa, sautéed vegetables, and Parmesan cheese. Season with salt and pepper.
4. Stuff each portobello mushroom with the quinoa mixture.
5. Bake for 20 minutes until mushrooms are tender and stuffing is golden brown.
6. Garnish with fresh basil and serve.

Nutrient Content (per serving):

- Calories: 250
- Total Fat: 10g
- Protein: 10g
- Carbohydrates: 20g
- Sugars: 5g
- Fiber: 5g
- Sodium: 250mg

Ingredient Tips:
These quinoa-stuffed portobello mushrooms are a hearty and nutritious dinner option, packed with fiber and plant-based protein.

TURKEY AND SPINACH STUFFED BELL PEPPERS

Servings: 4 | Prep Time: 15 mins | Cook Time: 40 mins | Carbs per Serving: 25g

INGREDIENTS

- 4 large bell peppers, tops cut off and seeds removed
- 1 tablespoon olive oil
- 1 pound ground turkey
- 1 small onion, diced
- 2 garlic cloves, minced
- 1 cup fresh spinach, chopped
- 1 cup cooked quinoa
- 1/2 cup tomato sauce (no added sugar)
- 1 teaspoon dried oregano
- 1 teaspoon dried basil
- Salt and pepper to taste
- 1/2 cup shredded mozzarella cheese (optional)

DIRECTIONS

1. Preheat oven to 375°F (190°C). Place bell peppers in a baking dish.
2. In a skillet over medium heat, heat olive oil. Add ground turkey, onion, and garlic. Cook until turkey is browned.
3. Stir in spinach and cook until wilted. Add cooked quinoa, tomato sauce, oregano, basil, salt, and pepper. Mix well.
4. Stuff each bell pepper with the turkey mixture. Top with shredded mozzarella cheese if using.
5. Cover with foil and bake for 30 minutes. Remove foil and bake for an additional 10 minutes until peppers are tender.
6. Serve hot.

Nutrient Content (per serving):

- Calories: 350
- Total Fat: 15g
- Protein: 25g
- Carbohydrates: 25g
- Sugars: 8g
- Fiber: 6g
- Sodium: 400mg

Ingredient Tips:
These turkey and spinach stuffed bell peppers are a filling and nutritious dinner option, featuring lean protein and fiber-rich quinoa and vegetables.

LEMON HERB GRILLED CHICKEN WITH BROWN RICE

Servings: 4 | Prep Time: 30 mins | Cook Time: 40 mins | Carbs per Serving: 35g

INGREDIENTS

- 4 boneless, skinless chicken breasts
- 1/4 cup olive oil
- Juice of 2 lemons
- 3 garlic cloves, minced
- 2 tablespoons fresh parsley, chopped
- 1 tablespoon fresh thyme, chopped
- Salt and pepper to taste
- 1 cup brown rice
- 2 cups water or low-sodium chicken broth
- 4 cups mixed vegetables (such as broccoli, carrots, and cauliflower)

DIRECTIONS

1. In a bowl, mix olive oil, lemon juice, garlic, parsley, thyme, salt, and pepper. Add chicken breasts and marinate for at least 30 minutes.
2. Cook brown rice: Rinse brown rice under cold water. In a medium pot, bring water or broth to a boil, add brown rice, reduce heat, cover, and simmer for 40 minutes until liquid is absorbed.
3. Steam vegetables: Place mixed vegetables in a steamer basket over boiling water, cover, and steam for about 5-7 minutes until tender.
4. Preheat grill to medium-high heat. Grill chicken for 6-7 minutes on each side until fully cooked.
5. Serve chicken with brown rice and steamed vegetables, garnished with additional lemon wedges if desired.

Nutrient Content (per serving):

- Calories: 450
- Total Fat: 15g
- Protein: 35g
- Carbohydrates: 35g
- Sugars: 5g
- Fiber: 6g
- Sodium: 200mg

Ingredient Tips:
A balanced dinner featuring lemon herb grilled chicken served with brown rice and steamed vegetables, providing a mix of protein, healthy fats, and fiber.

QUINOA & BLACK BEAN STUFFED SWEET POTATOES

Servings: 4 | Prep Time: 15 mins | Cook Time: 50 mins | Carbs per Serving: 55g

INGREDIENTS

- 4 medium sweet potatoes
- 1 tablespoon olive oil
- 1 cup cooked quinoa
- 1 can (14.5 oz) black beans, drained and rinsed
- 1 cup corn kernels (fresh or frozen)
- 1 small red onion, diced
- 1 red bell pepper, diced
- 2 garlic cloves, minced
- 1 teaspoon ground cumin
- 1 teaspoon chili powder
- Salt and pepper to taste
- 1/4 cup fresh cilantro, chopped
- Avocado slices (for garnish)
- Lime wedges (for serving)

DIRECTIONS

1. Preheat oven to 400°F (200°C). Pierce sweet potatoes with a fork and bake for 45-50 minutes until tender.
2. In a skillet, heat olive oil over medium heat. Add onion, bell pepper, and garlic. Sauté until soft.
3. Stir in cooked quinoa, black beans, corn, cumin, chili powder, salt, and pepper. Cook until heated through.
4. Once sweet potatoes are done, cut them in half lengthwise and scoop out some of the flesh to create a cavity.
5. Stuff each sweet potato with the quinoa and black bean mixture.
6. Garnish with fresh cilantro and avocado slices. Serve with lime wedges.

Nutrient Content (per serving):

- Calories: 450
- Total Fat: 10g
- Protein: 12g
- Carbohydrates: 55g
- Sugars: 10g
- Fiber: 12g
- Sodium: 300mg

Ingredient Tips:
These quinoa and black bean stuffed sweet potatoes are a delicious and fiber-rich dinner option, providing a balance of complex carbohydrates and plant-based protein.

GARLIC SHRIMP AND ZUCCHINI NOODLES

Servings: 4 | Prep Time: 10 mins | Cook Time: 10 mins | Carbs per Serving: 10g

INGREDIENTS

- 1 tablespoon olive oil
- 1 pound large shrimp, peeled and deveined
- 3 garlic cloves, minced
- 1/4 teaspoon red pepper flakes (optional)
- 4 medium zucchini, spiralized into noodles
- Juice of 1 lemon
- Salt and pepper to taste
- Fresh parsley, chopped (for garnish)
- Grated Parmesan cheese (optional)

DIRECTIONS

1. Heat olive oil in a large skillet over medium heat. Add garlic and red pepper flakes (if using). Cook for 1 minute until fragrant.
2. Add shrimp to the skillet and cook for 2-3 minutes on each side until pink and opaque.
3. Remove shrimp from the skillet and set aside.
4. In the same skillet, add spiralized zucchini noodles and cook for 2-3 minutes until slightly softened.
5. Return shrimp to the skillet, add lemon juice, salt, and pepper. Toss to combine.
6. Serve garnished with fresh parsley and grated Parmesan cheese if desired.

Nutrient Content (per serving):

- Calories: 220
- Total Fat: 10g
- Protein: 25g
- Carbohydrates: 10g
- Sugars: 5g
- Fiber: 3g
- Sodium: 450mg

Ingredient Tips:
A light and flavorful dinner of garlic shrimp served over zucchini noodles, providing a low-carb option packed with protein and healthy fats.

MOROCCAN-SPICED CHICKPEA AND SPINACH STEW

Servings: 4 | Prep Time: 10 mins | Cook Time: 20 mins | Carbs per Serving: 35g

INGREDIENTS

- 1 tablespoon olive oil
- 1 onion, diced
- 3 garlic cloves, minced
- 1 tablespoon fresh ginger, grated
- 1 teaspoon ground cumin
- 1 teaspoon ground coriander
- 1/2 teaspoon ground cinnamon
- 1/4 teaspoon cayenne pepper (optional)
- 1 can (14.5 oz) diced tomatoes (no added sugar)
- 1 can (14.5 oz) chickpeas, drained and rinsed
- 4 cups fresh spinach
- 1/4 cup fresh cilantro, chopped (for garnish)
- Cooked brown rice or quinoa for serving

DIRECTIONS

1. Heat olive oil in a large pot over medium heat. Add onion, garlic, and ginger. Sauté until onion is soft.
2. Stir in cumin, coriander, cinnamon, and cayenne pepper (if using). Cook for 1 minute until fragrant.
3. Add diced tomatoes and chickpeas. Bring to a simmer and cook for 10 minutes.
4. Stir in fresh spinach and cook until wilted, about 5 minutes.
5. Season with salt and pepper to taste. Garnish with fresh cilantro.
6. Serve with cooked brown rice or quinoa.

Nutrient Content (per serving):

- Calories: 250
- Total Fat: 8g
- Protein: 10g
- Carbohydrates: 35g
- Sugars: 8g
- Fiber: 10g
- Sodium: 300mg

Ingredient Tips:

This Moroccan-spiced chickpea and spinach stew is a flavorful and nutritious dinner option, rich in fiber and plant-based protein.

BAKED TILAPIA WITH TOMATO BASIL SAUCE

Servings: 4 | Prep Time: 10 mins | Cook Time: 15 mins | Carbs per Serving: 7g

INGREDIENTS

- 4 tilapia fillets
- 1 tablespoon olive oil
- Salt and pepper to taste
- 2 cups cherry tomatoes, halved
- 1/4 cup red onion, finely chopped
- 2 garlic cloves, minced
- 2 tablespoons fresh basil, chopped
- 1 tablespoon balsamic vinegar

DIRECTIONS

1. Preheat oven to 400°F (200°C). Place tilapia fillets on a baking sheet lined with parchment paper. Drizzle with olive oil and season with salt and pepper.
2. Bake for 12-15 minutes until tilapia is opaque and flakes easily with a fork.
3. While tilapia is baking, prepare the tomato basil sauce. In a bowl, combine cherry tomatoes, red onion, garlic, basil, and balsamic vinegar. Mix well.
4. Serve baked tilapia topped with the tomato basil sauce.

Nutrient Content (per serving):

- Calories: 220
- Total Fat: 8g
- Protein: 30g
- Carbohydrates: 7g
- Sugars: 4g
- Fiber: 2g
- Sodium: 250mg

Ingredient Tips:

Baked tilapia with a fresh tomato basil sauce is a light and delicious dinner option, providing lean protein and healthy fats.

CHICKEN AND VEGETABLE STIR-FRY

Servings: 4 | Prep Time: 15 mins | Cook Time: 15 mins | Carbs per Serving: 12g

INGREDIENTS

- 1 tablespoon olive oil
- 1 pound boneless, skinless chicken breasts, sliced into thin strips
- 1 red bell pepper, sliced
- 1 yellow bell pepper, sliced
- 1 cup snap peas
- 1 small broccoli crown, cut into florets
- 3 garlic cloves, minced
- 1 tablespoon fresh ginger, grated
- 3 tablespoons low-sodium soy sauce or tamari
- 1 tablespoon rice vinegar
- 1 tablespoon sesame oil
- 1 teaspoon sesame seeds (optional)

DIRECTIONS

1. Heat olive oil in a large skillet or wok over medium-high heat. Add chicken strips and cook until browned and cooked through, about 5-7 minutes. Remove chicken from skillet and set aside.
2. In the same skillet, add bell peppers, snap peas, and broccoli. Cook until vegetables are tender-crisp, about 5 minutes.
3. Add garlic and ginger, and cook for another minute.
4. Return chicken to the skillet. Add soy sauce, rice vinegar, and sesame oil. Toss to combine and heat through.
5. Serve hot, garnished with sesame seeds if desired.

Nutrient Content (per serving):

- Calories: 300
- Total Fat: 15g
- Protein: 28g
- Carbohydrates: 12g
- Sugars: 5g
- Fiber: 3g
- Sodium: 600mg

Ingredient Tips:
This chicken and vegetable stir-fry is a quick and easy dinner option, packed with protein and colorful vegetables, perfect for a balanced and nutritious meal.

SPICED LENTIL AND SWEET POTATO STEW

Servings: 4 | Prep Time: 10 mins | Cook Time: 25 mins | Carbs per Serving: 45g

INGREDIENTS

- 1 tablespoon olive oil
- 1 onion, diced
- 3 garlic cloves, minced
- 1 tablespoon fresh ginger, grated
- 1 teaspoon ground cumin
- 1 teaspoon ground coriander
- 1/2 teaspoon ground turmeric
- 1/4 teaspoon cayenne pepper (optional)
- 1 large sweet potato, peeled and diced
- 1 cup red lentils, rinsed
- 1 can (14.5 oz) diced tomatoes (no added sugar)
- 4 cups low-sodium vegetable broth
- 4 cups fresh spinach
- Salt and pepper to taste
- Fresh cilantro, chopped (for garnish)

DIRECTIONS

1. Heat olive oil in a large pot over medium heat. Add onion, garlic, and ginger. Sauté until onion is soft.
2. Stir in cumin, coriander, turmeric, and cayenne pepper (if using). Cook for 1 minute until fragrant.
3. Add sweet potato, red lentils, diced tomatoes, and vegetable broth. Bring to a boil, then reduce heat and simmer for 20-25 minutes until sweet potato and lentils are tender.
4. Stir in fresh spinach and cook until wilted, about 5 minutes.
5. Season with salt and pepper to taste. Garnish with fresh cilantro.
6. Serve hot.

Nutrient Content (per serving):

- Calories: 350
- Total Fat: 8g
- Protein: 15g
- Carbohydrates: 45g
- Sugars: 10g
- Fiber: 12g
- Sodium: 350mg

Ingredient Tips:
This spiced lentil and sweet potato stew is a hearty and nutritious dinner option, rich in fiber and plant-based protein, perfect for a warm and satisfying meal.

Chapter Ten

Diabetic Friendly Fish and Seafood Recipes

GRILLED SALMON WITH AVOCADO SALSA

Servings: 4 | Prep Time: 15 mins | Cook Time: 10 mins | Carbs per Serving: 12g

INGREDIENTS

- 4 salmon fillets (6 oz each)
- 1 tbsp olive oil
- Salt and pepper to taste
- 2 avocados, diced
- 1 small red onion, finely chopped
- 1 small jalapeno, seeded and finely chopped
- 1/4 cup fresh cilantro, chopped
- Juice of 2 limes
- 1/4 tsp cumin
- 1/4 tsp salt

DIRECTIONS

1. Preheat the grill to medium-high heat.
2. Brush salmon fillets with olive oil and season with salt and pepper.
3. Grill salmon for about 4-6 minutes per side, or until the fish flakes easily with a fork.
4. In a bowl, combine diced avocados, red onion, jalapeno, cilantro, lime juice, cumin, and salt.
5. Serve grilled salmon topped with avocado salsa.

Nutrient Content (per serving):

- Calories: 420
- Total Fat: 28g
- Protein: 35g
- Carbohydrates: 12g
- Sugars: 1g
- Fiber: 8g
- Sodium: 300mg

Ingredient Tips:

- Salmon: High in protein and omega-3 fatty acids, which are beneficial for heart health.
- Avocado: Low glycemic index and rich in healthy fats, which help in maintaining steady glucose levels.

LEMON GARLIC SHRIMP STIR-FRY

Servings: 4 | Prep Time: 10 mins | Cook Time: 15 mins | Carbs per Serving: 8g

INGREDIENTS

- 1 lb large shrimp, peeled and deveined
- 2 tbsp olive oil
- 4 cloves garlic, minced
- 1 red bell pepper, sliced
- 1 yellow bell pepper, sliced
- 1 zucchini, sliced
- Juice of 1 lemon
- 1 tbsp fresh parsley, chopped
- Salt and pepper to taste

DIRECTIONS

1. Heat olive oil in a large skillet over medium-high heat.
2. Add garlic and sauté until fragrant.
3. Add shrimp and cook until pink, about 2-3 minutes per side.
4. Remove shrimp from the skillet and set aside.
5. Add bell peppers and zucchini to the skillet and sauté until tender, about 5-7 minutes.
6. Return shrimp to the skillet, add lemon juice, parsley, salt, and pepper. Toss to combine and heat through.
7. Serve immediately.

Nutrient Content (per serving):

- Calories: 240
- Total Fat: 12g
- Protein: 28g
- Carbohydrates: 8g
- Sugars: 4g
- Fiber: 3g
- Sodium: 460mg

Ingredient Tips:

- Shrimp: A low-calorie protein source that helps in maintaining blood sugar levels.
- Vegetables: Low glycemic index vegetables like bell peppers and zucchini add fiber and nutrients.

BAKED COD WITH QUINOA AND KALE

Servings: 4 | Prep Time: 10 mins | Cook Time: 25 mins | Carbs per Serving: 22g

INGREDIENTS

- 4 cod fillets (6 oz each)
- 2 tbsp olive oil
- 1 lemon, sliced
- 1 tsp dried thyme
- Salt and pepper to taste
- 1 cup quinoa
- 2 cups water
- 4 cups kale, chopped
- 2 cloves garlic, minced

DIRECTIONS

1. Preheat oven to 375°F (190°C).
2. Place cod fillets in a baking dish, drizzle with olive oil, and top with lemon slices, thyme, salt, and pepper.
3. Bake for 15-20 minutes, or until the fish is opaque and flakes easily with a fork.
4. Meanwhile, rinse quinoa and cook in 2 cups of water according to package instructions.
5. In a skillet, sauté garlic in olive oil until fragrant, then add kale and cook until wilted.
6. Serve baked cod with quinoa and sautéed kale.

Nutrient Content (per serving):
- Calories: 370
- Total Fat: 12g
- Protein: 35g
- Carbohydrates: 22g
- Sugars: 1g
- Fiber: 4g
- Sodium: 180mg

Ingredient Tips:
- Cod: A lean source of protein that is low in fat and calories.
- Quinoa: A high-protein, low-glycemic grain that helps maintain steady blood sugar levels.

TUNA AND CHICKPEA SALAD

Servings: 4 | Prep Time: 15 mins | Cook Time: 0 mins | Carbs per Serving: 18g

INGREDIENTS

- 2 cans tuna in water, drained
- 1 can chickpeas, drained and rinsed
- 1 small red onion, finely chopped
- 1 cucumber, diced
- 1 red bell pepper, diced
- 1/4 cup fresh parsley, chopped
- 3 tbsp olive oil
- Juice of 1 lemon
- Salt and pepper to taste

DIRECTIONS

1. In a large bowl, combine tuna, chickpeas, red onion, cucumber, bell pepper, and parsley.
2. In a small bowl, whisk together olive oil, lemon juice, salt, and pepper.
3. Pour dressing over the salad and toss to combine.
4. Serve chilled or at room temperature.

Nutrient Content (per serving):
- Calories: 280
- Total Fat: 14g
- Protein: 25g
- Carbohydrates: 18g
- Sugars: 3g
- Fiber: 6g
- Sodium: 420mg

Ingredient Tips:
- Tuna: High in protein and omega-3 fatty acids, beneficial for heart health and glucose management.
- Chickpeas: Provide fiber and protein, contributing to stable blood sugar levels.

MEDITERRANEAN BAKED HALIBUT

Servings: 4 | Prep Time: 10 mins | Cook Time: 25 mins | Carbs per Serving: 6g

INGREDIENTS

- 4 halibut fillets (6 oz each)
- 2 tbsp olive oil
- 1 cup cherry tomatoes, halved
- 1/2 cup Kalamata olives, pitted and sliced
- 2 cloves garlic, minced
- 1 tbsp fresh oregano, chopped
- Juice of 1 lemon
- Salt and pepper to taste

DIRECTIONS

1. Preheat oven to 375°F (190°C).
2. Place halibut fillets in a baking dish, drizzle with olive oil, and top with cherry tomatoes, olives, garlic, oregano, lemon juice, salt, and pepper.
3. Bake for 20-25 minutes, or until the fish is opaque and flakes easily with a fork.
4. Serve hot, garnished with additional fresh oregano if desired.

Nutrient Content (per serving):

- Calories: 320
- Total Fat: 18g
- Protein: 32g
- Carbohydrates: 6g
- Sugars: 2g
- Fiber: 2g
- Sodium: 460mg

Ingredient Tips:

- Halibut: A lean source of protein and omega-3 fatty acids.
- Olives: Provide healthy fats and antioxidants, contributing to heart health and stable glucose levels.

SHRIMP AND VEGETABLE SKEWERS

Servings: 4 | Prep Time: 15 mins | Cook Time: 10 mins | Carbs per Serving: 10g

INGREDIENTS

- 1 lb large shrimp, peeled and deveined
- 1 red bell pepper, cut into chunks
- 1 yellow bell pepper, cut into chunks
- 1 zucchini, sliced
- 1 red onion, cut into chunks
- 2 tbsp olive oil
- 2 cloves garlic, minced
- Juice of 1 lemon
- 1 tbsp fresh parsley, chopped
- Salt and pepper to taste

DIRECTIONS

1. Preheat grill to medium-high heat (or preheat oven to 400°F/200°C).
2. In a large bowl, toss shrimp and vegetables with olive oil, garlic, lemon juice, parsley, salt, and pepper.
3. Thread shrimp and vegetables onto skewers.
4. Grill for 3-4 minutes per side, or bake for 10-12 minutes, until shrimp are cooked through and vegetables are tender.
5. Serve immediately.

Nutrient Content (per serving):

- Calories: 220
- Total Fat: 10g
- Protein: 24g
- Carbohydrates: 10g
- Sugars: 4g
- Fiber: 3g
- Sodium: 380mg

Ingredient Tips:

- Shrimp: High in protein and low in calories, beneficial for maintaining stable glucose levels.
- Vegetables: Low glycemic index and high in fiber, contributing to steady energy levels.

SEARED SCALLOPS WITH QUINOA PILAF

Servings: 4 | Prep Time: 15 mins | Cook Time: 20 mins | Carbs per Serving: 26g

INGREDIENTS

- 1 lb sea scallops
- 2 tbsp olive oil
- Salt and pepper to taste
- 1 cup quinoa
- 2 cups water
- 1 small carrot, diced
- 1 celery stalk, diced
- 1/2 cup peas
- 2 green onions, chopped
- 1 tbsp fresh parsley, chopped

DIRECTIONS

1. Rinse quinoa and cook in 2 cups of water according to package instructions.
2. In a skillet, heat 1 tbsp olive oil and sauté carrot, celery, and peas until tender. Stir in cooked quinoa, green onions, and parsley. Keep warm.
3. Pat scallops dry with paper towels, then season with salt and pepper.
4. Heat remaining olive oil in a skillet over medium-high heat. Sear scallops for about 2-3 minutes per side until golden brown and opaque.
5. Serve seared scallops over quinoa pilaf.

Nutrient Content (per serving):

- Calories: 350
- Total Fat: 12g
- Protein: 28g
- Carbohydrates: 26g
- Sugars: 3g
- Fiber: 5g
- Sodium: 340mg

Ingredient Tips:

- Scallops: High in protein and low in fat, making them a great choice for glucose management.
- Quinoa: A complete protein with a low glycemic index, contributing to steady energy levels.

HERB-CRUSTED BAKED TILAPIA

Servings: 4 | Prep Time: 10 mins | Cook Time: 20 mins | Carbs per Serving: 5g

INGREDIENTS

- 4 tilapia fillets (6 oz each)
- 1/4 cup almond flour
- 1/4 cup grated Parmesan cheese
- 1 tbsp fresh parsley, chopped
- 1 tbsp fresh basil, chopped
- 1 tbsp fresh thyme, chopped
- 2 tbsp olive oil
- Salt and pepper to taste
- Lemon wedges for serving

DIRECTIONS

1. Preheat oven to 400°F (200°C).
2. In a bowl, combine almond flour, Parmesan cheese, parsley, basil, thyme, salt, and pepper.
3. Brush tilapia fillets with olive oil and coat with the herb mixture.
4. Place fillets on a baking sheet and bake for 15-20 minutes, or until the fish flakes easily with a fork.
5. Serve with lemon wedges.

Nutrient Content (per serving):

- Calories: 310
- Total Fat: 18g
- Protein: 32g
- Carbohydrates: 5g
- Sugars: 1g
- Fiber: 2g
- Sodium: 320mg

Ingredient Tips:

- Tilapia: A lean protein source that helps in maintaining stable blood sugar levels.
- Almond Flour: Low glycemic index and rich in healthy fats and fiber.

SPICY GRILLED MACKEREL WITH BROWN RICE

Servings: 4 | Prep Time: 10 mins | Cook Time: 25 mins | Carbs per Serving: 24g

INGREDIENTS

- 4 mackerel fillets (6 oz each)
- 2 tbsp olive oil
- 2 tsp paprika
- 1 tsp cumin
- 1 tsp chili powder
- 1 tsp garlic powder
- 1 cup brown rice
- 2 cups water
- Salt and pepper to taste

DIRECTIONS

1. Rinse brown rice and cook in 2 cups of water according to package instructions.
2. In a small bowl, mix paprika, cumin, chili powder, garlic powder, salt, and pepper.
3. Brush mackerel fillets with olive oil and coat with the spice mixture.
4. Preheat grill to medium-high heat and grill mackerel for about 4-6 minutes per side, or until the fish flakes easily with a fork.
5. Serve grilled mackerel with brown rice.

Nutrient Content (per serving):

- Calories: 410
- Total Fat: 22g
- Protein: 30g
- Carbohydrates: 24g
- Sugars: 0g
- Fiber: 3g
- Sodium: 290mg

Ingredient Tips:

- Mackerel: High in omega-3 fatty acids, which are beneficial for heart health and glucose management.
- Brown Rice: A whole grain with a low glycemic index, contributing to steady blood sugar levels.

COCONUT CURRY SHRIMP WITH CAULIFLOWER RICE

Servings: 4 | Prep Time: 15 mins | Cook Time: 15 mins | Carbs per Serving: 12g

INGREDIENTS

- 1 lb large shrimp, peeled and deveined
- 2 tbsp coconut oil
- 1 onion, chopped
- 2 cloves garlic, minced
- 1 tbsp ginger, grated
- 1 tbsp curry powder
- 1 can (14 oz) coconut milk
- 1 cup cherry tomatoes, halved
- 1 head cauliflower, grated into rice-sized pieces
- 1/4 cup fresh cilantro, chopped
- Salt and pepper to taste

DIRECTIONS

1. Heat coconut oil in a large skillet over medium heat. Sauté onion, garlic, and ginger until fragrant.
2. Add curry powder and cook for another minute.
3. Stir in coconut milk and cherry tomatoes, then simmer for 5 minutes.
4. Add shrimp and cook until pink and cooked through, about 5 minutes.
5. In a separate skillet, sauté cauliflower rice in a bit of coconut oil until tender, about 5 minutes.
6. Serve coconut curry shrimp over cauliflower rice, garnished with fresh cilantro.

Nutrient Content (per serving):

- Calories: 360
- Total Fat: 24g
- Protein: 28g
- Carbohydrates: 12g
- Sugars: 4g
- Fiber: 5g
- Sodium: 420mg

Ingredient Tips:

- Shrimp: High in protein and low in calories, helping to maintain stable glucose levels.
- Cauliflower Rice: A low-carb alternative to traditional rice, with a low glycemic index.

Chapter Eleven

Diabetic Friendly Poultry Recipes

LEMON HERB GRILLED CHICKEN

Servings: 4 | Prep Time: 10 mins | Cook Time: 15 mins | Carbs per Serving: 1g

INGREDIENTS

- 4 boneless, skinless chicken breasts
- 1/4 cup olive oil
- 1/4 cup fresh lemon juice
- 2 cloves garlic, minced
- 1 tablespoon fresh rosemary, chopped
- 1 tablespoon fresh thyme, chopped
- Salt and pepper to taste

DIRECTIONS

1. In a bowl, whisk together olive oil, lemon juice, garlic, rosemary, thyme, salt, and pepper.
2. Place chicken breasts in a shallow dish and pour marinade over them. Cover and refrigerate for at least 30 minutes.
3. Preheat grill to medium-high heat.
4. Grill chicken for 6-7 minutes on each side, or until fully cooked.
5. Serve hot with a side of steamed vegetables.

Nutrient Content (per serving):

- Calories: 260
- Total Fat: 14g
- Protein: 28g
- Carbohydrates: 1g
- Sugars: 0g
- Fiber: 0g
- Sodium: 75mg

Ingredient Tips:
Lemon juice is low glycemic and adds a refreshing flavor without spiking blood sugar levels.

BAKED CHICKEN AND QUINOA STUFFED PEPPERS

Servings: 4 | Prep Time: 15 mins | Cook Time: 35 mins | Carbs per Serving: 22g

INGREDIENTS

- 4 large bell peppers, tops cut off and seeds removed
- 1 cup cooked quinoa
- 2 cups cooked, shredded chicken breast
- 1/2 cup chopped tomatoes
- 1/2 cup black beans, drained and rinsed
- 1/4 cup chopped fresh cilantro
- 1 teaspoon cumin
- 1 teaspoon chili powder
- Salt and pepper to taste

DIRECTIONS

1. Preheat oven to 375°F (190°C).
2. In a large bowl, mix together quinoa, chicken, tomatoes, black beans, cilantro, cumin, chili powder, salt, and pepper.
3. Stuff each bell pepper with the chicken and quinoa mixture.
4. Place stuffed peppers in a baking dish and cover with foil.
5. Bake for 30-35 minutes, until peppers are tender.

Nutrient Content (per serving):

- Calories: 310
- Total Fat: 6g
- Protein: 30g
- Carbohydrates: 22g
- Sugars: 6g
- Fiber: 6g
- Sodium: 400mg

Ingredient Tips:
Quinoa is a great alternative grain with a low glycemic index and high fiber content, helping to manage blood sugar levels.

CHICKEN AVOCADO SALAD

Servings: 4 | Prep Time: 15 mins | Cook Time: 0 mins | Carbs per Serving: 6g

INGREDIENTS

- 2 cups cooked, shredded chicken breast
- 1 ripe avocado, diced
- 1/4 cup red onion, finely chopped
- 1/4 cup celery, diced
- 1/4 cup plain Greek yogurt
- 1 tablespoon fresh lime juice
- Salt and pepper to taste

DIRECTIONS

1. In a large bowl, combine chicken, avocado, red onion, and celery.
2. In a small bowl, mix Greek yogurt, lime juice, salt, and pepper.
3. Pour yogurt mixture over the chicken mixture and toss to combine.
4. Serve immediately or chill until ready to serve.

Nutrient Content (per serving):

- Calories: 250
- Total Fat: 15g
- Protein: 23g
- Carbohydrates: 6g
- Sugars: 1g
- Fiber: 3g
- Sodium: 200mg

Ingredient Tips:
Avocado is a great source of healthy fats that help keep you full and stabilize blood sugar levels.

SPICY CHICKEN LETTUCE WRAPS

Servings: 4 | Prep Time: 10 mins | Cook Time: 15 mins | Carbs per Serving: 8g

INGREDIENTS

- 1 lb ground chicken
- 1 tablespoon olive oil
- 1 red bell pepper, diced
- 1 small onion, diced
- 2 cloves garlic, minced
- 1 tablespoon soy sauce (low sodium)
- 1 tablespoon sriracha sauce
- 1 head of butter lettuce, leaves separated

DIRECTIONS

1. Heat olive oil in a large skillet over medium heat.
2. Add ground chicken, bell pepper, onion, and garlic. Cook until chicken is browned and vegetables are tender.
3. Stir in soy sauce and sriracha sauce. Cook for an additional 2 minutes.
4. Spoon chicken mixture into lettuce leaves and serve.

Nutrient Content (per serving):

- Calories: 210
- Total Fat: 11g
- Protein: 22g
- Carbohydrates: 8g
- Sugars: 3g
- Fiber: 2g
- Sodium: 400mg

Ingredient Tips:
Lettuce wraps are a great low-carb alternative to traditional wraps, helping to maintain steady blood sugar levels.

COCONUT CURRY CHICKEN

Servings: 4 | Prep Time: 10 mins | Cook Time: 25 mins | Carbs per Serving: 6g

INGREDIENTS

- 1 lb chicken thighs, cut into bite-sized pieces
- 1 tablespoon coconut oil
- 1 onion, chopped
- 2 cloves garlic, minced
- 1 tablespoon ginger, minced
- 1 can (14 oz) coconut milk
- 1 tablespoon curry powder
- 1 cup chopped spinach
- Salt and pepper to taste

DIRECTIONS

1. Heat coconut oil in a large skillet over medium heat.
2. Add onion, garlic, and ginger. Sauté until fragrant.
3. Add chicken and cook until browned.
4. Stir in coconut milk and curry powder. Simmer for 15-20 minutes, until chicken is cooked through.
5. Add spinach and cook until wilted.
6. Season with salt and pepper to taste.

Nutrient Content (per serving):

- Calories: 350
- Total Fat: 28g
- Protein: 22g
- Carbohydrates: 6g
- Sugars: 2g
- Fiber: 2g
- Sodium: 150mg

Ingredient Tips:
Coconut milk provides healthy fats that help maintain satiety and stabilize blood sugar levels.

BALSAMIC GLAZED CHICKEN WITH ROASTED VEGETABLES

Servings: 4 | Prep Time: 15 mins | Cook Time: 30 mins | Carbs per Serving: 12g

INGREDIENTS

- 4 boneless, skinless chicken breasts
- 1/4 cup balsamic vinegar
- 2 tablespoons olive oil
- 2 tablespoons honey (optional)
- 2 cups broccoli florets
- 1 red bell pepper, sliced
- 1 zucchini, sliced
- Salt and pepper to taste

DIRECTIONS

1. Preheat oven to 400°F (200°C).
2. In a bowl, mix balsamic vinegar, olive oil, honey, salt, and pepper.
3. Place chicken breasts in a baking dish and pour balsamic mixture over them. Marinate for 15 minutes.
4. On a baking sheet, arrange broccoli, bell pepper, and zucchini. Drizzle with olive oil and season with salt and pepper.
5. Place chicken and vegetables in the oven and bake for 25-30 minutes, until chicken is cooked through and vegetables are tender.

Nutrient Content (per serving):

- Calories: 320
- Total Fat: 14g
- Protein: 32g
- Carbohydrates: 12g
- Sugars: 7g
- Fiber: 3g
- Sodium: 300mg

Ingredient Tips:
Balsamic vinegar adds a rich flavor without adding too many carbohydrates, helping to manage blood sugar levels.

CHICKEN AND VEGETABLE STIR-FRY

Servings: 4 | Prep Time: 10 mins | Cook Time: 15 mins | Carbs per Serving: 8g

INGREDIENTS

- 1 lb chicken breast, sliced into thin strips
- 1 tablespoon sesame oil
- 2 cups mixed vegetables (e.g., bell peppers, broccoli, snap peas)
- 2 cloves garlic, minced
- 1 tablespoon soy sauce (low sodium)
- 1 teaspoon ginger, minced
- 1 tablespoon sesame seeds (optional)

DIRECTIONS

1. Heat sesame oil in a large skillet or wok over medium-high heat.
2. Add chicken and cook until browned.
3. Add garlic and ginger, and sauté until fragrant.
4. Add mixed vegetables and cook until tender-crisp.
5. Stir in soy sauce and cook for an additional 2 minutes.
6. Sprinkle with sesame seeds if desired and serve immediately

Nutrient Content (per serving):

- Calories: 250
- Total Fat: 10g
- Protein: 28g
- Carbohydrates: 8g
- Sugars: 3g
- Fiber: 3g
- Sodium: 350mg

Ingredient Tips:
Using a variety of vegetables adds fiber and nutrients without increasing the glycemic load.

HERB-ROASTED CHICKEN THIGHS

Servings: 4 | Prep Time: 10 mins | Cook Time: 40 mins | Carbs per Serving: 2g

INGREDIENTS

- 8 chicken thighs, bone-in, skin-on
- 2 tablespoons olive oil
- 1 tablespoon fresh rosemary, chopped
- 1 tablespoon fresh thyme, chopped
- 1 tablespoon fresh parsley, chopped
- 1 lemon, sliced
- Salt and pepper to taste

DIRECTIONS

1. Preheat oven to 425°F (220°C).
2. In a bowl, mix olive oil, rosemary, thyme, parsley, salt, and pepper.
3. Rub the mixture over the chicken thighs and place them in a roasting pan.
4. Arrange lemon slices around the chicken.
5. Roast in the oven for 35-40 minutes, until the chicken is golden and cooked through.

Nutrient Content (per serving):

- Calories: 400
- Total Fat: 28g
- Protein: 34g
- Carbohydrates: 2g
- Sugars: 0g
- Fiber: 0g
- Sodium: 200mg

Ingredient Tips:
Chicken thighs are higher in fat than breasts, providing a more satiating meal that can help keep blood sugar levels steady.

CHICKEN AND LENTIL SOUP

Servings: 6 | Prep Time: 15 mins | Cook Time: 35 mins | Carbs per Serving: 24g

INGREDIENTS

- 1 lb chicken breast, diced
- 1 cup green lentils, rinsed
- 1 onion, chopped
- 2 carrots, diced
- 2 celery stalks, diced
- 3 cloves garlic, minced
- 6 cups low-sodium chicken broth
- 1 teaspoon cumin
- 1 teaspoon turmeric
- 1 teaspoon paprika
- Salt and pepper to taste

DIRECTIONS

1. In a large pot, sauté onion, carrots, celery, and garlic until softened.
2. Add chicken and cook until browned.
3. Stir in lentils, chicken broth, cumin, turmeric, paprika, salt and pepper.
4. Bring to a boil, then reduce heat and simmer for 30-35 minutes, until lentils are tender.
5. Serve hot.

Nutrient Content (per serving):

- Calories: 280
- Total Fat: 4g
- Protein: 32g
- Carbohydrates: 24g
- Sugars: 4g
- Fiber: 10g
- Sodium: 250mg

Ingredient Tips:
Lentils are a great source of fiber and have a low glycemic index, making them ideal for blood sugar management.

MEDITERRANEAN CHICKEN BAKE

Servings: 4 | Prep Time: 10 mins | Cook Time: 30 mins | Carbs per Serving: 6g

INGREDIENTS

- 4 boneless, skinless chicken breasts
- 1/4 cup olive oil
- 1/4 cup balsamic vinegar
- 1 cup cherry tomatoes, halved
- 1/2 cup Kalamata olives, pitted and sliced
- 1/4 cup feta cheese, crumbled
- 2 cloves garlic, minced
- 1 teaspoon dried oregano
- Salt and pepper to taste

DIRECTIONS

1. Preheat oven to 375°F (190°C).
2. In a small bowl, mix olive oil, balsamic vinegar, garlic, oregano, salt, and pepper.
3. Place chicken breasts in a baking dish and pour the olive oil mixture over them.
4. Top with cherry tomatoes, olives, and feta cheese.
5. Bake for 25-30 minutes, or until chicken is cooked through and cheese is slightly browned.
6. Serve hot, garnished with fresh herbs if desired.

Nutrient Content (per serving):

- Calories: 320
- Total Fat: 20g
- Protein: 29g
- Carbohydrates: 6g
- Sugars: 3g
- Fiber: 2g
- Sodium: 450mg

Ingredient Tips:
Kalamata olives and feta cheese add healthy fats and a savory flavor, contributing to satiety and balanced blood sugar levels.

Chapter Twelve

Barbara Lost Diabetic 28-Day Meal Plan, Grocery List and Shopping Guide

WEEK 1: DR BARBARA' LOST DIABETIC MEAL PLAN

	BREAKFAST	LUNCH	DINNER	SNACKS
MON	Spinach and Feta Omelette	Quinoa and Black Bean Salad	Grilled Lemon Herb Chicken with Quinoa	Greek Yogurt with Chia Seeds and Berries
TUES	Avocado and Egg Breakfast Bowl	Lentil and Vegetable Soup	Spaghetti Squash with Turkey Bolognese	Almond Butter and Celery Sticks
WED	Quinoa Breakfast Skillet	Spelt Berry and Veggie Bowl	Lentil and Vegetable Stew	Spiced Roasted Chickpeas
THURS	Greek Yogurt with Nuts and Seeds	Chickpea and Spinach Stew	Baked Salmon with Asparagus and Quinoa	Avocado and Black Bean Salsa
FRI	Mushroom and Spinach Breakfast Burrito	Brown Rice and Veggie Stir-Fry	Stuffed Bell Peppers with Ground Beef	Spiced Roasted Nuts
SAT	Spinach and Mushroom Egg Scramble	Quinoa Stuffed Bell Peppers	Chickpea and Spinach Curry	Greek Yogurt with Nuts and Seeds
SUN	Quinoa Breakfast Bowl	Spinach and Feta Stuffed Mushrooms	Baked Cod with Tomato and Olive Relish	Edamame Hummus with Veggie Sticks

WEEK 2 : DR BARBARA' LOST DIABETIC MEAL PLAN

	BREAKFAST	LUNCH	DINNER	SNACKS
MON	Avocado and Egg Rye Toast	Mediterranean Chickpea Salad	Quinoa-Stuffed Portobello Mushrooms	Spiced Chickpea and Avocado Toast
TUES	Chickpea and Veggie Breakfast Hash	Baked Salmon with Quinoa and Asparagus	Turkey and Spinach Stuffed Bell Peppers	Greek Yogurt with Chia Seeds and Berries
WED	Smoked Salmon and Avocado Bowl	Black Bean and Avocado Wrap	Lemon Herb Grilled Chicken with Brown Rice	Almond Butter and Celery Sticks
THURS	Spicy Black Bean and Egg Breakfast Wrap	Kale & Quinoa Salad with Lemon-Tahini Dressing	Quinoa & Black Bean Stuffed Sweet Potatoes	Spiced Roasted Chickpeas
FRI	Lentil and Spinach Breakfast Stew	Spelt and Lentil Pilaf	Garlic Shrimp and Zucchini Noodles	Avocado and Black Bean Salsa
SAT	Tofu Scramble with Vegetables	Avocado and Chickpea Stuffed Sweet Potatoes	Moroccan-Spiced Chickpea and Spinach Stew	Spiced Roasted Nuts
SUN	Spelt Flour Savory Pancakes	Brown Rice and Veggie Sushi Rolls	Baked Tilapia with Tomato Basil Sauce	Greek Yogurt with Nuts and Seeds

WEEK 3 : DR BARBARA' LOST DIABETIC MEAL PLAN

	BREAKFAST	LUNCH	DINNER	SNACKS
MON	Kamut and Vegetable Stir-Fry	Greek Yogurt Parfait with Berries and Nuts	Chicken and Vegetable Stir-Fry	Edamame Hummus with Veggie Sticks
TUES	Egg and Vegetable Muffins	Roasted Veggie and Hummus Bowl	Spiced Lentil and Sweet Potato Stew	Spiced Chickpea and Avocado Toast
WED	Oatmeal with Savory Toppings	Curried Chickpea and Spinach Stew	Grilled Lemon Herb Chicken with Quinoa	Greek Yogurt with Chia Seeds and Berries
THURS	Breakfast Stuffed Bell Peppers	Quinoa and Black Bean Stuffed Tomatoes	Spaghetti Squash with Turkey Bolognese	Almond Butter and Celery Sticks
FRI	Baked Avocado with Egg	Lentil and Vegetable Soup	Lentil and Vegetable Stew	Spiced Roasted Chickpeas
SAT	Broccoli and Cheese Breakfast Casserole	Spelt Berry and Veggie Bowl	Baked Salmon with Asparagus and Quinoa	Avocado and Black Bean Salsa
SUN	Cauliflower Breakfast Rice	Chickpea and Spinach Stew	Stuffed Bell Peppers with Ground Beef	Spiced Roasted Nuts

WEEK 4 : DR BARBARA' LOST DIABETIC MEAL PLAN

	BREAKFAST	LUNCH	DINNER	SNACKS
MON	Quinoa Breakfast Bowl	Brown Rice and Veggie Stir-Fry	Chickpea and Spinach Curry	Greek Yogurt with Nuts and Seeds
TUES	Millet Porridge with Spinach and Mushrooms	Quinoa Stuffed Bell Peppers	Baked Cod with Tomato and Olive Relish	Edamame Hummus with Veggie Sticks
WED	Buckwheat Breakfast Bowl	Spinach and Feta Stuffed Mushrooms	Quinoa-Stuffed Portobello Mushrooms	Spiced Chickpea and Avocado Toast
THURS	Chia Seed Pudding with Almonds and Berries	Mediterranean Chickpea Salad	Turkey and Spinach Stuffed Bell Peppers	Greek Yogurt with Chia Seeds and Berries
FRI	Savory Amaranth Breakfast Porridge	Baked Salmon with Quinoa and Asparagus	Lemon Herb Grilled Chicken with Brown Rice	Almond Butter and Celery Sticks
SAT	Sweet Potato and Black Bean Breakfast Hash	Black Bean and Avocado Wrap	Quinoa & Black Bean Stuffed Sweet Potatoes	Spiced Roasted Chickpeas
SUN	Spinach and Tofu Scramble	Kale & Quinoa Salad with Lemon-Tahini Dressing	Garlic Shrimp and Zucchini Noodles	Avocado and Black Bean Salsa

GROCERY SHOPPING LIST FOR DR BARBARA' LOST DIABETIC MEAL PLAN

MEAT & SEAFOOD

Eggs	Chicken Breast	Cod
Greek Yogurt	Turkey Ground	Shrimp
Tofu	Salmon	

GRAINS & LEGUMES

Quinoa	Oats	Black Beans
Brown Rice	Millet	Chickpeas
Spelt	Buckwheat	Lentils
Farro	Amaranth	Kamut

VEGETABLES

Spinach	Tomatoes	Avocado
Mushrooms	Sweet Potatoes	Cucumbers
Bell Peppers	Cauliflower	Carrots
Asparagus	Broccoli	Celery
Zucchini	Kale	Mixed Greens

FRUITS

Berries (Blueberries, Strawberries, Raspberries)	Grapefruit	Lemon

HEALTHY FATS

Olive Oil	Nuts (Almonds, Walnuts)	Seeds (Chia Seeds, Flaxseeds)

HEALTHY FATS

Feta Cheese	Edamame	Tahini
Cheese (for casserole)	Hummus	Almond Butter

SHOPPING GUIDE FOR DR BARBARA' LOST DIABETIC MEAL PLAN

1. **Plan Ahead:** Review the meal plan for the upcoming week and make a shopping list. Check your pantry and fridge to see what you already have.
2. **Stick to the Perimeter:** Fresh produce, dairy, and proteins are usually found around the edges of the grocery store. Focus on these sections to find the freshest ingredients.
3. **Buy in Bulk:** For grains, legumes, and seeds, buying in bulk can be cost-effective. Just make sure to store them properly to keep them fresh.
4. **Choose Organic:** Whenever possible, choose organic produce and proteins to avoid genetically modified ingredients.
5. **Fresh is Best:** While frozen vegetables can be a good backup, fresh vegetables provide the best nutrients and flavor.
6. **Read Labels:** For packaged items like Greek yogurt and hummus, read the labels to avoid added sugars and unnecessary ingredients.
7. **Weekly Shopping:** Plan to shop weekly to ensure you have fresh ingredients, especially for perishable items like vegetables and fruits.

By following this meal plan and shopping guide, you'll be well on your way to managing diabetes through delicious, nutritious meals inspired by Barbara O'Neil's teachings. Enjoy the journey to better health!

Chapter Thirteen

Conclusion

Embarking on the journey to manage diabetes through diet can feel overwhelming, but "Dr. Barbara Lost Diabetic Cookbook - Barbara O'Neil's 28-Day Meal Plan & Natural Recipes Reversing Diabetes" has been designed to make this process both manageable and enjoyable. By integrating Barbara O'Neil's profound insights into a practical and delicious meal plan, this cookbook provides the tools necessary to maintain stable blood sugar levels, reduce cravings, and sustain steady energy throughout the day.

Throughout these pages, you have discovered a variety of recipes that rely on low glycemic foods, high fiber content, and healthy fats. Each meal, snack, and dessert has been carefully crafted to support diabetes management and overall health. By focusing on natural, unprocessed ingredients and avoiding refined sugars and genetically modified foods, you are giving your body the nourishment it needs to thrive.

As you progress through the 30-day meal plan, remember that consistency is key. The recipes in this cookbook are not just for a month—they are designed to become a sustainable part of your lifestyle. By embracing these dietary principles, you can make lasting changes that will benefit your health for years to come.

Whether you are new to Barbara O'Neil's teachings or a longtime follower, this cookbook serves as a valuable resource. The inclusion of her treasured recipes, some of which are no longer available online, ensures that her wisdom remains accessible to all. By following the meal plan and using the shopping guide, you are well-equipped to take control of your diabetes and improve your overall well-being.

As you continue on this journey, remember that you are not alone. Many people have successfully managed their diabetes through dietary changes, and you can too. Use this cookbook as your guide, and take comfort in knowing that each meal you prepare is a step toward better health. Enjoy the delicious, nutritious dishes and the benefits they bring to your life.

Here's to a future of balanced glucose levels, reduced cravings, and steady energy. Here's to living a healthier, more fulfilling life. Enjoy the journey and the delicious recipes along the way!

Index 1: The 2024 Dirty Dozen™ and Clean Fifteen™

The Dirty Dozen and the Clean Fifteen™ refer to lists compiled by the Environmental Working Group (EWG), an organization dedicated to environmental health. They analyze data from the USDA and FDA regarding pesticide residues in commercial crops. These lists help consumers make informed choices about buying organic versus conventional produce based on pesticide levels.

The Dirty Dozen includes fruits and vegetables with the highest pesticide loads, while the Clean Fifteen™ comprises produce with lower pesticide residues. It's essential to note that even items on the Clean Fifteen™ may still have pesticide residues, so thorough washing is advised.

Since these lists are updated annually, it's crucial to check the latest version before grocery shopping.
Visit www.ewg.org/FoodNews for the most recent lists and a comprehensive guide to pesticides in produce.

DIRTY DOZEN™	CLEAN FIFTEEN™
◯ Strawberries	◯ Carrots
◯ Spinach	◯ Sweet Potatoes
◯ Kale, collard & mustard greens	◯ Mangoes
◯ Grapes	◯ Mushrooms
◯ Peaches	◯ Watermelon
◯ Pears	◯ Cabbage
◯ Nectarines	◯ Kiwi
◯ Apples	◯ Honeydew melon
◯ Bell & hot Peppers	◯ Asparagus
◯ Cherries	◯ Sweet peas (frozen)
◯ Blueberries	◯ Papaya*
◯ Green Beans	◯ Onions
	◯ Pineapple
	◯ Sweet corn*
	◯ Avocados

Index 2: Measurement Conversions

Volume Equivalents (Liquid)

US STANDARD	US STANDARD (OUNCES)	METRIC (APPROXIMATE)
2 tablespoons	1 fl. oz.	30 mL
¼ cup	2 fl. oz.	60 mL
½ cup	4 fl. oz.	120 mL
1 cup	8 fl. oz.	240 mL
1½ cups	12 fl. oz.	355 mL
2 cups or 1 pint	16 fl. oz.	475 mL
4 cups or 1 quart	32 fl. oz.	1 L
1 gallon	128 fl. oz.	4 L

Volume Equivalents (Dry)

US STANDARD	METRIC (APPROXIMATE)
⅛ teaspoon	0.5 mL
¼ teaspoon	1 mL
½ teaspoon	2 mL
¾ teaspoon	4 mL
1 teaspoon	5 mL
1 tablespoon	15 mL
¼ cup	59 mL
⅓ cup	79 mL
½ cup	118 mL
⅔ cup	156 mL
¾ cup	177 mL
1 cup	235 mL
2 cups or 1 pint	475 mL
3 cups	700 mL
4 cups or 1 quart	1 L

Oven Temperatures

FAHRENHEIT	CELSIUS (APPROXIMATE)
250°F	120°C
300°F	150°C
325°F	165°C
350°F	180°C
375°F	190°C
400°F	200°C
425°F	220°C
450°F	230°C

Weight Equivalents

FAHRENHEIT	CELSIUS (APPROXIMATE)
½ ounce	15g
1 ounce	30g
2 ounces	60g
4 ounces	115g
8 ounces	225g
12 ounces	340g
16 ounces or 1 pound	455g

Index 3: Recipe Index

A
- Almond Butter and Celery Sticks. 54
- Almond Flour Chocolate Chip Cookies, 61
- Almond Flour Pumpkin Muffins, 4
- Avocado and Black Bean Salsa, 55
- Avocado and Chickpea Stuffed Sweet Potatoes, 35
- Avocado and Egg Breakfast Bowl, 13
- Avocado and Egg Rye Toast, 17
- Avocado and Kale Salad, 41
- Avocado Chocolate Mousse, 59, 62

B
- Baked Apple with Cinnamon and Almonds, 60
- Baked Avocado with Egg, 22
- Baked Chicken and Quinoa Stuffed Peppers, 81
- Baked Cod with Quinoa and Kale, 76
- Baked Cod with Tomato and Olive Relish, 69
- Baked Salmon with Asparagus and Quinoa, 67
- Baked Salmon with Quinoa and Asparagus, 33
- Baked Tilapia with Tomato Basil Sauce, 72
- Balsamic Glazed Chicken with Roasted Vegetables, 83
- Berry Yogurt Parfait, 64
- Black Bean and Avocado Wrap, 33
- Black Bean and Quinoa Soup, 48
- Breakfast Recipes, 12
- Breakfast Stuffed Bell Peppers, 22
- Broccoli and Almond Soup, 50
- Broccoli and Cheese Breakfast Casserole, 23
- Brown Rice and Edamame Salad, 42
- Brown Rice and Veggie Stir-Fry, 31
- Brown Rice and Veggie Sushi Rolls, 35
- Buckwheat Breakfast Bowl, 25
- Butternut Squash and Red Lentil Soup, 47

C
- Carrot and Ginger Soup, 50
- Cauliflower Breakfast Rice, 23
- Chia Seed Pudding with Almonds and Berries, 25
- Chia Seed Pudding with Berries, 59
- Chia Seed Pudding with Berries, 62
- Chicken and Lentil Soup, 85
- Chicken and Vegetable Soup, 47
- Chicken and Vegetable Stir-Fry, 73, 84
- Chicken Avocado Salad, 82
- Chickpea and Spinach Curry, 68
- Chickpea and Spinach Soup, 49
- Chickpea and Spinach Stew, 30
- Chickpea and Veggie Breakfast Hash, 17
- Cinnamon Walnut Baked Apples, 63
- Coconut Curry Chicken, 83
- Coconut Curry Shrimp with Cauliflower Rice, 79
- Coconut Flour Lemon Bars, 63
- Coconut Yogurt Parfait, 60
- Curried Chickpea and Spinach Stew, 38

D
- Desserts Recipes, 58
- Dinner Recipes, 65

E
- Edamame Hummus with Veggie Sticks, 57
- Egg and Vegetable Muffins, 21

F
- Farro and Arugula Salad, 44
- Farro and Vegetable Breakfast Bowl, 27
- Fish and Seafood Recipes, 74

G
- Garlic Shrimp and Zucchini Noodles, 71
- Greek Yogurt and Cucumber Salad, 42
- Greek Yogurt Parfait with Berries and Nuts, 36,
- Greek Yogurt with Chia Seeds and Berries, 54
- Greek Yogurt with Nuts and Seeds, 14, 16, 56
- Grilled Lemon Herb Chicken with Quinoa, 66
- Grilled Salmon with Avocado Salsa, 75

H
- Herb-Crusted Baked Tilapia, 78
- Herb-Roasted Chicken Thighs, 84

K
- Kale & Quinoa Salad with Lemon-Tahini Dressing, 34
- Kale and Cannellini Bean Soup, 49
- Kale and White Bean Soup, 51
- Kamut and Vegetable Stir-Fry, 20

L
- Lemon Blueberry Yogurt Bark, 61
- Lemon Garlic Shrimp Stir-Fry, 75
- Lemon Herb Grilled Chicken, 81
- Lemon Herb Grilled Chicken with Brown Rice, 70
- Lentil and Spinach Breakfast Stew, 19
- Lentil and Spinach Soup, 46
- Lentil and Vegetable Salad, 41
- Lentil and Vegetable Soup, 29
- Lentil and Vegetable Stew, 67
- Lunch Recipes, 28

M
- Mediterranean Baked Halibut, 77
- Mediterranean Chicken Bake, 85
- Mediterranean Chickpea Salad, 32, 44
- Millet Porridge with Spinach and Mushrooms, 24
- Moroccan-Spiced Chickpea and Spinach Stew, 72
- Mushroom and Barley Soup, 51
- Mushroom and Spinach Breakfast Burrito, 15

O
- Oatmeal with Savory Toppings, 21

Q
- Quinoa & Black Bean Stuffed Sweet Potatoes, 71
- Quinoa and Black Bean Salad, 29, 40
- Quinoa and Black Bean Stuffed Tomatoes, 38
- Quinoa and Vegetable Soup, 46
- Quinoa Breakfast Bowl, 16, 24
- Quinoa Breakfast Skillet, 14
- Quinoa Stuffed Bell Peppers, 31
- Quinoa-Stuffed Portobello Mushrooms, 69

R
- Roasted Beet and Lentil Salad, 43
- Roasted Veggie and Hummus Bowl, 36, 37

O
- Oatmeal with Savory Toppings, 21

S

- Salad Recipes, 39
- Savory Amaranth Breakfast Porridge, 26
- Seared Scallops with Quinoa Pilaf, 78
- Shrimp and Vegetable Skewers, 77
- Smoked Salmon and Avocado Bowl, 18
- Snacks Recipes, 53
- Soup Recipes, 45
- Spaghetti Squash with Turkey Bolognese, 66
- Spelt and Avocado Salad, 43
- Spelt and Lentil Pilaf, 34
- Spelt Berry and Veggie Bowl, 30
- Spelt Flour Savory Pancakes, 20
- Spiced Chickpea and Avocado Toast, 56
- Spiced Lentil and Sweet Potato Stew, 73
- Spiced Roasted Chickpeas, 55
- Spiced Roasted Nuts, 57
- Spicy Black Bean and Egg Breakfast Wrap, 18
- Spicy Chicken Lettuce Wraps, 82
- Spicy Grilled Mackerel with Brown Rice, 79
- Spinach and Chickpea Salad, 40
- Spinach and Feta Omelette, 13
- Spinach and Feta Stuffed Mushrooms, 32
- Spinach and Mushroom Egg Scramble, 15
- Spinach and Tofu Scramble, 27
- Stuffed Bell Peppers with Ground Beef, 68
- Sweet Potato and Black Bean Breakfast Hash, 26
- Sweet Potato and Black Bean Soup, 52

T

- Tofu Scramble with Vegetables, 19
- Tomato and White Bean Soup, 48
- Tuna and Chickpea Salad, 76
- Turkey and Spinach Stuffed Bell Peppers, 70

Z

- Zucchini and Chickpea Soup, 52

Printed in the USA
CPSIA information can be obtained
at www.ICGtesting.com
LVHW061953020924
789880LV00012B/1181

9 798333 481900